THE OTHER SIDE OF THE FIREWALL

The Real-Life Stories of Movers, Shakers, & Glass Ceiling Breakers in Cybersecurity

Ryan Williams Sr.

ISBN: 979-8-9989796-0-6
Printed in the United States of America

Dedication

To every guest who graciously shared their story on *The Other Side of the Firewall*, thank you. Your honesty, perseverance, and insight gave this guide its spark. To my cohosts both past and present, Shannon Tynes, LeVon Maynard, Chris Abacon, and Daniel Acevedo, your dedication and presence kept the show grounded and growing. To my wife, Chamire, and kids, Aiyana, Ryan Jr., and Mason, thank you for your patience, support, and inspiration. And to the countless career switchers, veterans, students, and aspiring cyber professionals—this guide is for you. Keep going. You're closer than you think.

Disclaimer

This guide was born from real conversations with real people navigating unconventional paths into cybersecurity. It's not a silver bullet—but it is a mirror, a compass, and a source of community. My hope is that these stories show you what's possible and inspire you to take the next step—whether that's pursuing a certification, applying for a new role, or finding a mentor. The door is open—you just have to walk through it.

Watch the full interviews on our YouTube playlist:
"The Other Side of the Firewall: The Real-Life Stories of Movers, Shakers, & Glass Ceiling Breakers in Cybersecurity":
https://www.youtube.com/playlist?list=PLfVugeH-1uZo22ZSNFsUQJ6iNE-DiZ3DV

TABLE OF CONTENTS

PREFACE
No Cap, Just Facts

I'm here to dispel the rumors and nonsense. The snake oil salesmen, the "get rich overnight" shenanigans. The "take this eight-week course and land a six-figure job" BS.

Cybersecurity—the profession—is a tough gig. No doubt about it. A lot of people are getting curious because of social media clickbait and YouTube theater. Is the money good? Yes. Are the days long? Sometimes. It depends on the role. Can you get rich quick? Maybe. But it depends on how much you're willing to sell out.

Are there many people of color, women, neurodivergent folks, or veterans in cybersecurity?

No. Not nearly enough.

This space is still heavily populated primarily by white men. And that's a hard, honest truth.

This guide? It's about the other truths, the ones that rarely get told.

These are the real stories. Of people of color. Women. Neurodivergent professionals. Veterans and career switchers. Each person sat with me on *The Other Side of the Firewall* podcast to share what it really took. Their sacrifices, their struggles, and their missteps. Their inspirations, their triumphs, and their wisdom gained by doing the hard things—again and again.

This isn't hype. This is a collection of excellence. Passed directly to you, the reader, the learner, the builder. Use it to break in. Use it to beat the odds. Use it to take up space and prosper, just like the guests featured here.

Let's get it!

—Ryan Williams Sr., MS-CIA, CISSP, PMP
Host of *The Other Side of the Firewall Podcast*
CEO of RAM Cyber Consulting & Assessments, LLC.

INTRODUCTION
Against All Odds

Thre is no such thing as a linear path into cybersecurity. Some of us come from IT. Others come into the field through law, medicine, law enforcement, theater, human resources, business— you name it. How you arrive isn't nearly as important as what you do once you break in. And because the barrier to entry is so high, the moment you're in, you must make an impact. If not for yourself, then for the ones still pounding on the glass trying to get through.

I often joke with friends that I beat the odds. Most folks are born into a social class and either stay there or slip lower. Upward mobility is almost nonexistent for many Americans. According to the Brookings Institution, 54 percent of Black men born into the poorest fifth of the

1

income distribution remain in that lowest fifth as adults, compared to just 22 percent of white men. That's not just a stat; it's a systemic reality.

And yet, somehow, I've lived three lifetimes. I was born below the poverty line. At around nine or ten years old, I graduated from being poor to being broke. And somewhere in my thirties, I climbed into the middle class. In my forties, I had the audacity to retire from one career and start fresh. This time as an entrepreneur.

All stories have a beginning. Mine may feel familiar or entirely different from yours, but either way, I hope it encourages you. After four decades, my life feels like something out of a film. Not because I escaped poverty, but because my children have no concept of what it means to be poor— monetarily or mentally. It's one thing to lack money. It's another to have a lack of hope. I may have lacked the former, but I never gave up the latter.

So, let's rewind.

I was born in the summer of 1983 at Buffalo's children's hospital. My parents were both undergraduates at Canisius University, and I was raised in the Kensington-Bailey area, specifically in Langfield Homes— one of the city's public housing developments. Today, the community remains Buffalo's third poorest, with more than 58 percent of residents living below the federal poverty line and a median annual income of just $17,011, according to 2020 census data. My mom went into labor during my grandmother's birthday party and managed to hold off delivering me until the following day. My birth certificate read "Baby Boy Rhone"— my mother's maiden name. My father didn't show up until days later and never signed the certificate.

That tiny omission wouldn't mean much until I applied for my first government passport decades later. I had to explain to a senior admin

2

that I wouldn't be asking my estranged father for a favor just to check a box. I was embarrassed I hadn't noticed the missing signature sooner, but I reasoned that if the Department of Defense could trust me with a top-secret clearance at nineteen, the Department of State could make a few concessions, too. I still carry that chip on my shoulder. A lack of a father figure shaped many of my decisions, from study habits to marriage to fatherhood. Anybody can learn from good examples. It takes a sharp eye to learn from the bad ones.

My mother grew up in modest conditions, too. She was one of five kids and the only one to go to college. She enlisted in the Army as a vehicle mechanic shortly after I was born and had to drop out one semester shy of graduating. Officer commissioning was on the table, but diapers and a steady paycheck took precedence. She taught me work ethic, responsibility, and to look people square in the eye when speaking. To this day, my wife and podcast cohost, Shannon Tynes, say I need to ease up on eye contact. I guess I can come across as intense to strangers. I also now realize eye contact for some can be uncomfortable, so I've learned to "read the room."

My father was the youngest of three college-educated brothers raised by a sharecropper turned entrepreneur. His mother died of cancer early in his life, which I suspect left its own scar. He would complete his degree in accounting and all three of his children, including me, would go on to complete a degree or two of our own. When less than 3 percent of Black men held degrees in my paternal grandfather's era, we've turned a generational struggle into a legacy of academic achievement. I should also mention that my father is the reason I love video games. When I was about four or five, he showed up with a Nintendo Entertainment System (NES) and a tiny thirteen-inch wood-paneled tube TV. That

NES ignited a lifelong passion for gaming and brought joy to the red-brick projects that provided limited other options.

I wasn't necessarily set up for success, though. What I lacked in inheritance, I made up for in grit—and a solid friend group. My mother, in trying to make ends meet, entrusted me to my grandmother while she served in the Army. My grandmother lived on a fixed income in the projects and raised me with the kind of strength that doesn't get put in history books. She walked me to school every day, rain or shine, until she befriended my best friend James's mother, Mrs. Kearney, better known to us grade-schoolers as "Mrs. Bonnie." I can still hear the sound the snow made when it crunched under my dress shoes on our long walks through blizzards. James and I met in kindergarten; he sat across the table from me pouring Elmer's glue in his palm and peeling it off like dead skin. He also wore a Cowboys Starter jacket to and from school. You know we were good friends if I could let such an offense slide for almost four decades straight. His family gave me a second home and suburban stability I'll never forget, or ever repay.

At school, I was the shy, skinny kid with big glasses, a lisp, and a love of R. L. Stine books, video games, and anime. I stayed on the honor roll until high school, when numbers and letters started to team up in unholy ways. But even then, I loved learning.

I bounced between Catholic schools—St. James, then St. Aloysius, and finally Turner-Carroll High. Each one closed its doors not long after I passed through. Not saying I was the reason, but hey, a coincidence?

High school brought its own growing pains but also my first taste of IT. My friend James and I were recruited to help cable a school computer lab in 2000. Let's just say I cut more than cable—I needed stitches in my hand. Still, it sparked something. I dreamed of becoming a computer scientist, even if math tried to hold me back.

That same year, I met the love of my life, Chamire. Beautiful, smart, and driven. I didn't know it at the time, but I would need her courage and strength every step of the way of our future Air Force journey, building our amazing family through retirement, and then on to entrepreneurship. But I'm getting ahead of myself.

I applied to several colleges. Most passed. Alfred University accepted me as a computer science major. Canisius accepted me under general studies. I declined Canisius out of pride and pretense. I wanted to go away, thinking I knew what was best. But just before heading off to Alfred, I found out I needed a cosigner for the loans. My mother said no.

I was crushed. But that "no" was one of the greatest gifts I've ever received.

I regrouped, pivoted to Erie Community College, worked full-time at HSBC bank, and hustled through the brutal Buffalo winters. Still, something was missing. I craved purpose, opportunity, and escape. So, after some soul-searching—and a blunt comment from my best friend, quoting the opening line of the second verse in 50 Cent's "Wanksta"— I walked right into the Air Force recruiter's office.

My path into the Air Force wasn't seamless, but it was ordained. I started Basic in March 2003. That's where everything changed. And that, my friend, is where the cybersecurity origin story begins.

In late March 2003, I boarded a plane to Lackland Air Force Base in San Antonio, Texas. It was only the second time I'd ever flown, and the first time I'd left New York for anywhere other than Canada. Over the next six weeks, I got my ass kicked. It wasn't the yelling—that was familiar territory. My mom, an Army vet, could out-yell and out-stare any training instructor. It was the exhaustion, the relentless running, the uncertainty, and the newness of being completely outside my element that got to me.

During training, we were offered a few job selections. One of them was telephone maintenance. They lined us up next to telephone poles, one behind the other. Each time someone climbed and came down, they handed off the harness to the next person. When it was my turn, I got maybe halfway up the pole before realizing something deep and fundamental: I don't do heights. I couldn't even let go with both hands to lean back like they asked. Back on the ground, the sergeant gave me an earful and marked me unqualified. That left two open jobs—biomedical technology and data maintenance technician.

I landed in data maintenance, and it turned out to be the perfect pivot. I spent the next seven months at Keesler Air Force Base in Biloxi, Mississippi, learning how to run cables, punch down panels, create Ethernet and crossover cables, build PCs, configure switches and routers, and manage telephone systems. I learned the foundations of what would become my life's work.

My first duty station was Mountain Home Air Force Base in Idaho. I worked on Tactical Air Operations Modules—think air traffic control in a box—and deployed to Balad, Iraq, where I narrowly missed daily mortar and rocket attacks. That deployment taught me more about fear, focus, and fragility than any textbook ever could.

From there, I was stationed in Anchorage, Alaska, at Joint Base Elmendorf-Richardson on an NSA assignment. I leveled up. I learned tech control, fiber fabrication, asynchronous transfer mode systems, and SONET rings. More importantly, I learned to lead. I took over the help desk, sharpened my IT skills, and finally saw myself as a professional, someone who belonged.

Next was Langley AFB in Virginia. It was a baptism by fire. I helped manage the Air Force's global network boundary, which was over 500 switches and routers across 120 bases, both domestic and abroad. I led a team of thirty-three airmen and eleven contractors, and together, we upgraded the Air Force's aging infrastructure. It was during this time that I met Shannon, LeVon, and Daniel, who became my future podcast cohosts.

Then came the assignment that changed everything: Joint Communications Support Element (JCSE) in Tampa, Florida. JCSE is where the military's most capable communicators come to play. It's where I honed not just my network skills but also added satellite communications, virtualization, Active Directory, radio work, and full-spectrum IT support to my toolkit. I worked alongside special operations, three-letter agencies, task forces I still can't name, and coalition forces. I saw the world—Germany, Sicily, Morocco, Israel, and the Netherlands—and gained a global perspective.

It was at JCSE that I earned my PMP, CISSP, CEH, and ultimately completed my master's in cybersecurity and information assurance. I also met Chris Abacon and two of my favorite mentors: CMSgt (Ret.) Chris Jones and MSG (Ret.) Jeff Lodick, both of whom you'll learn more about in this guide.

My final military stop was Incirlik Air Base in Turkey. It was there, in the middle of a pandemic lockdown, that I launched this podcast. Two weeks of mandatory quarantine gave me time to reflect. I called up Shannon and LeVon, and we brainstormed how we could speak to our strengths and shine a spotlight on people of color in cybersecurity as platforms like that were few and far between. We didn't have it all figured out, but we had passion. And that was enough to hit *record*.

When I retired from the military, I took a position at a data privacy firm in Georgia. There, I was mentored by Marine veteran Steve Haley, who helped me understand just how transferable my skills were. Almost a year in, I pivoted to a small veteran-owned contracting firm out of Illinois providing services to the US Department of Housing and Urban Development.

That opportunity came full circle. I had grown up in public housing, and now I was helping protect the systems that served people like me. But when the second Trump administration stood up the Department of Government Efficiency, our contract was abruptly terminated.

I could've been bitter, but faith stepped in again. Chris Jones put in a word for me, and I landed a new role at a Fortune 500 company in financial services. Today, I work in corporate risk management, specifically in organizational resiliency oversight. In plain language, I help make sure the business can keep moving through any disruption—from cybersecurity attacks to natural disasters.

I didn't follow a straight line to get here. I stumbled, I pivoted, I doubled back. But every step mattered. Every "no" led to a better "yes." And now, my mission is to light the path for others. Not as someone who had it all figured out, but as someone who refused to quit.

This is my story. And I share it not to impress you but to remind you that your own path, however messy, can still lead to something extraordinary.

You belong here.

A Moment of Reflection:

Where did your story begin, and what experiences shaped your early view of success? Reflect on how your upbringing, community, or family dynamics influenced your work ethic or dreams. What messages, spoken or unspoken, did you absorb about what's possible for someone like you?

What roadblocks or detours have redirected your path, and how did you respond to them? Think about a time you were told "no" or a door closed unexpectedly. What did you learn about yourself in that moment? What doors opened because of it?

Who has shown up for you as a mentor, ally, or supporter? And how did they make a difference? Consider how mentorship or sponsorship helped you break into new spaces. What characteristics made those people memorable? In what ways can you be that person for someone else now?

What chips do you carry on your shoulder, and how do they push you forward? Think about moments where doubt, exclusion, or past experiences created a need to prove yourself. What fuels you in the hard times? How do you balance your fire with rest, healing, and joy?

What systems or cycles do you want to help dismantle for the next generation? Have you broken any generational barriers, whether it's poverty or something else entirely?

PART I: LEGACY AND LEADERSHIP

"If you can see it, then you can be it."

For some, positive images and role models are around every corner—on magazine covers, billboards, and television ads. For others, the search is harder. For would-be cyber professionals, the representation is ... mixed.

If you're looking for a *Mr. Robot* or *Jason Bourne* of cybersecurity, you'll have to dig deeper. Find the newsletters, the Twitter threads, the Discord groups, and the podcasts. That's where we live.

Black and brown technologists, women in cyber, veterans, and neurominorities not only exist in this space—they thrive. They carry with them legacies of resilience, leadership, and transformation. The people featured in this guide are not exceptions; they're proof.

> **"Please don't call me a unicorn; I may be rare, but I'm real."**
> **—Ieshea Hollins**

CHAPTER 1

From the Block to the Boardroom

E veryone has an origin story, but not everyone chooses to lead by example. Just ask Charles Barkley. In the early nineties, Nike ran a now-famous ad campaign. Barkley, one of the greatest to ever play the game of basketball, stared directly into the camera and said, "I am not a role model. Just because I dunk a basketball doesn't mean I should raise your kids." He wasn't wrong.

But in cybersecurity, especially for people of color and marginalized groups, we don't always get the luxury of opting out of leadership. The world sees us. The world watches us. So, when we rise, we often carry the hopes of a whole community.

Thankfully, we've got leaders who accept the challenge and carry that weight with grace.

Dr. Joseph J. Burt-Miller Jr.

Ask A CISSP | Meet Dr. Joseph J. Burt-Miller Jr. - Season 2 Episode 10

Dr. Joseph J. Burt-Miller Jr. enters the conversation already walking with intention. He doesn't arrive with the résumé first. He shows up with respect, community ties, and a spirit of giving. His journey begins in Mount Vernon, New York, a place that carries both the memory and momentum of his origin. It's the same Mount Vernon that gave birth to Oscar-winning actor and activist Denzel Washington, as well as music icons Heavy D & The Boyz, Al B. Sure!, Pete Rock, and Pharoahe Monch. That place never left him. It walks with him into rooms he once thought were off-limits.

Before the cyber badges and doctorate title, Dr. Burt-Miller turned wrenches, not firewalls, as a US Air Force HVAC specialist. His cyber origin story didn't start in a lab or a lecture hall. It started with aching knees and older coworkers showing up to the job with more physical wear than they should've had to bear.

Military occupational health studies and data from the Defense Centers for Public Health indicate that musculoskeletal disorders are more common among HVAC specialists in the military than in many other Air Force specialties. Chronic back, shoulder, and knee problems brought on by frequent lifting, bending, and climbing—sometimes in dangerous situations with little ergonomic support—are included in this. Their limping into work served as a wake-up call as much as an act of sympathy. He said, "I don't want that to be me," and it wasn't.

13

What followed was a story that too many of us know well: studying during lunch breaks, facing rejection after rejection when applying for IT roles, and questioning if he was good enough. He studied hard enough that his HVAC supervisor nicknamed him "Professor." The grind didn't feel glamorous. It felt lonely. But he kept going. And when someone finally gave him a chance, he didn't waste it. That first supervisor who saw something in him became a lifelong mentor. That kind of mentorship is sacred. The kind where someone sees you before you become who you're meant to be.

As Dr. Burt-Miller transitioned into IT and later cyber, he didn't forget the rooms that denied him entry. Instead of resentment, he brought receipts in the form of experience, growth, and gratitude. He worked across government systems, such as VA hospitals, the DoD Cyber Crime Center, Homeland Security, and finally the NSA. But even as his positions grew more technical, his purpose became more personal.

Earning a doctorate wasn't for clout. It wasn't to teach or for a title. It was to finish something that mattered to him, because his grandmother gave him the kind of simple but life-altering wisdom that only elders can: "You don't finish anything you don't start." He took those words and built a legacy from them.

The study hall came next, born from necessity, accountability, and a refusal to let others fail in silence. When he struggled to prepare for the PMP exam, he didn't isolate himself. He created space. He gathered strangers on LinkedIn into a small collective who bombed practice exams together, grew together, and eventually passed together. That study hall now has over eight hundred members. And one of those early members changed his entire family's life by landing a role at Amazon.

That's not just test prep; that's economic justice, Black excellence in motion, and community uplift in real time.

Dr. Burt-Miller understands that mentorship isn't a one-time event. It's a rhythm, a relationship, a responsibility. He now finds himself being reached out to instead of being the one doing the reaching. That reversal is not lost on him; it humbles him and empowers him at the same time.

He's not content with just being a success story. He's building something for others to walk through. His podcast, *Cyber Coffee Hour*, cohosted with Alfredzo Nash, is set to give a voice to professionals who were once invisible in the field. Their goal is simple but radical: Let Black and brown folks see themselves in cyber. Let Mount Vernon, and neighborhoods like it, know that cyber belongs to them, too.

What he desires is to demystify the career path, make the vocabulary accessible, and normalize faces like his in places such as the NSA, boardrooms, and bootcamps. He's not performing for diversity stats, rather he's reclaiming tech as a place where we've always belonged, even if we've been pushed to the margins.

He mentors because he was mentored. He builds community because he once had to build himself back up after disappointment. He teaches because he knows what it's like to almost give up.

You don't finish anything you don't start. And Dr. Burt-Miller started a movement, whether he calls it that or not. It's visible. It's intentional. And it's growing.

If you're listening to his story thinking, "I don't have what it takes," remember this: he didn't either, at first. But he kept going. And so can you.

A Moment of Reflection:

1. What's one skill from your current or past role that others might overlook, but you believe could transfer well into cybersecurity or tech?

   Think about Dr. Burt-Miller's HVAC background and how he connected that mechanical mindset to systems thinking in cyber.

2. Have you ever felt discouraged during a transition or career pivot? What kept you moving forward—or what could help you keep going next time?

   Dr. Burt-Miller almost gave up before breaking into IT. Reflect on your own "almost gave up" moments.

3. What's a personal mantra or piece of advice that's stuck with you, like his grandmother's words, "You don't finish anything you don't start"?

   Write it down. If you don't have one, create your own.

4. What's one way you can give back—today or this month—through mentoring, encouragement, or resource sharing, just like Dr. Burt-Miller has done with his study hall and podcast?

   Think small: a comment, a repost, a check-in, a coffee chat.

5. If you launched a learning community like Dr. Burt-Miller's *DRJJBMJ Study Hall*, what would you call it, and who would it serve?

   Let yourself dream for a moment. This is about envisioning your impact.

16

Daryl Brooks

Ask A CISSP | Meet Daryl Brooks - Ask A CISSP Season 2 Episode 4

Daryl Brooks is a newly minted CISSP with over twenty years in the federal government and a deep-rooted passion for cybersecurity that didn't follow the traditional trajectory. His story resonates with anyone who's ever felt stuck behind a closed door, waiting for an opportunity that never came. Rather than continuing to wait, Daryl picked the locks of those doors through relentless self-improvement, education, and networking.

His interest in tech began early, though he hesitated to embrace it openly during high school. It wasn't until college at Delaware State University, an HBCU, that he embraced his path. Working at the academic computing office exposed him to real-world tech issues. He helped students with login issues and system access, which sparked a genuine love for IT. With encouragement from his mother, he majored in management information systems. He later pursued a graduate degree in information security management from Bowie State University, another HBCU.

Throughout college, he took full advantage of internship opportunities in federal agencies. From project management at the US Park Police to hands-on work at the FTC involving HVAC systems and network cabling, each experience helped Daryl inch closer to the cybersecurity field. He realized his long-term goal wasn't fixing computers; it was protecting information, infrastructure, and people.

17

After graduation, he landed a full-time position at the Social Security Administration (SSA). Despite a strong start, the role wasn't directly in cybersecurity, and over time, complacency crept in. He describes those early years as a comfortable but unfulfilling period. His stable career lacked the challenge and passion he craved. It wasn't until 2015 that he reignited his drive. Motivated by personal goals—like home ownership, marriage, and family planning—he relentlessly pursued certifications. After multiple failed attempts at the A+ and Network+ exams, he finally passed the A+ on his third try. That success became the momentum he needed. From 2015 onward, he amassed certifications like Security+, Project+, ITIL, and eventually CySA+.

During that period, he pivoted his SSA role to focus more on access management, handling privilege management, user provisioning, and identity life cycle. He also secured a detail with the internal security audit team, exposing him to governance, risk, and compliance (GRC). Though he wasn't yet in a full-on cybersecurity role, he was building his toolkit with intention.

Eventually, he took a risk, investing seven thousand in a CISSP bootcamp that turned out to be a poor fit. The program didn't suit his learning style, but that experience taught him a valuable lesson: you can't shortcut your goals by throwing money at them. So, he leaned into his tried-and-true method: practice exams, pattern recognition, and understanding how questions relate to real-world scenarios. His disciplined approach, paired with lessons from his background in sports, leadership, and family, carried him forward.

Networking played a crucial role in his ultimate pivot. A connection through his wife helped him get his résumé in front of a hiring manager at a federal agency. That led to a new role more aligned with his long-term goals. His story reinforces the value of networking—not just with professionals who look like you, but with people embedded in the systems you want to join.

Outside of work, Daryl is a family man who's rekindled his love for running after a health scare. Dropping fifteen pounds, he's found joy in reclaiming old habits. He also enjoys gaming, traveling, and going to the movies, with *The Super Mario Bros. Movie*, *M3GAN*, and *The Menu* as his most-recent watches. He doesn't just talk tech; he lives a balanced life, and his humility, humor, and wisdom shine through in every anecdote.

Daryl closes with heartfelt advice: don't underestimate any opportunity, no matter how small. Find extracurricular activities that challenge and stretch you. Leverage your faith, your past victories, and your support system to keep moving forward. And above all else, don't quit. You may be much closer to your goal than you think.

He recommends the book *The Proximity Principle* by Ken Coleman, a guide for leveraging strategic relationships to get where you want to be. And for those wondering how to connect? He's active on LinkedIn— look him up under "Daryl Brooks, CISSP."

This episode is more than a career roadmap; it's a testament to what happens when preparation meets persistence and when Black excellence is given space to thrive.

A Moment of Reflection:

1. **Daryl spoke about the power of community and mentorship in his cybersecurity journey.**

    How have mentors or community members supported your growth—and if you haven't had that yet, where might you begin to seek that support?

2. **He emphasized building transferable skills before officially entering the field.**

    What non-cybersecurity experience do you have (e.g., military, retail, teaching, or IT support) that could be reframed as a strength in your transition into cybersecurity?

3. **Daryl's work in helping others break into tech demonstrates servant leadership.**

    How can you "send the elevator back down" even as you're climbing? What small actions can you take today to help someone else?

4. **He navigated complex personal and professional decisions while staying grounded in purpose.**

    What is your "why" for entering cybersecurity? How can you keep that front and center when things get hard?

5. **Daryl did not wait until he had "arrived" to share what he knew—he built as he climbed.**

    What can you teach or share now—even if you're still learning—that could empower others to follow behind you?

Kenneth Ellington

Ask A CISSP | Meet Kenneth Ellington - The Other Side of the Firewall Season 2 Episode 1

Building a Resilient Cybersecurity Pipeline Ft. Kenneth Ellington, Founder of ECA Season 3

Kenneth Ellington's journey into the world of cybersecurity wasn't conventional. It was born of perseverance, family guidance, and a desire to give back to his community. Hailing from Tampa, Florida, Kenneth didn't just study cybersecurity, he lived it, transitioning from a high school deli worker at Publix to a cyber consultant and, ultimately, the founder and CEO of the Ellington Cyber Academy (ECA).

The pandemic brought a sudden halt to Kenneth's college graduation, no walk across the stage, no family celebration. But it didn't stop his momentum. Armed with a cybersecurity degree from the University of South Florida, he took a leap of faith and moved to Dallas, Texas, for his first professional role. Alone, away from family, and during the uncertainty of COVID-19, he embraced the discomfort and grew from it.

Despite early setbacks, including a canceled interview after buying his first suit, Kenneth stayed committed. "I've always been a very salty person," he jokes. But his drive, his fire, kept him pushing forward. He capitalized on relationships, like the one with a Publix manager who introduced him to the company's head of cybersecurity. That single connection changed his life, earning him an internship and validating the saying that "preparation meets opportunity."

Kenneth is passionate about representation. When he walked into his first security conference, he noticed only a handful of Black professionals, igniting something within him. "I saw the gap," he recalls, "and I wanted to bridge it." This became the foundation of the Ellington Cyber Academy, which trains individuals who are primarily people of color in niche cybersecurity fields like security information and event management (SIEM) and security orchestration, automation, and response (SOAR).

What began as a free training course he led for Blacks In Cybersecurity evolved into a formal business model after the students insisted they'd pay for his instruction. Within a year, he had formed a legitimate company with structured six-month programs, personalized coaching, hands-on labs, and hiring manager capstones. He focused on technical acumen as well as soft skills and confidence-building, something often overlooked in tech spaces.

As ECA matured, Kenneth recognized a powerful synergy: education could lead to placement. He bid for government contracts, with an aim to create employment pipelines for his graduates. His vision is bigger than just certs; it's about economic empowerment.

With the guidance of mentors like Fox Wade and inspired by his own father's journey in government contracting, Kenneth positioned ECA to become both a training ground and a contract fulfillment center, where students are taught, mentored, and hired—all under one roof. In just under two years, ECA had already placed students in competitive roles, contributing to over $250,000 in new salaries, and hit $100,000 in sales within the first quarter of 2025.

His goal for 2025 is two million dollars in signed government contracts. And he's putting in the groundwork now.

For someone so focused on cybersecurity and entrepreneurship, Kenneth's personal life is refreshingly balanced. He trains in kickboxing for stress relief and confidence, loves cooking (his original dream was to become a chef before he switched to cybersecurity), and jokes that if things go well, he might still go to culinary school one day.

Anime is another thing that brings him joy, especially titles like *Demon Slayer*, *My Hero Academia*, and *Blue Lock*. He appreciates the storytelling and how it hypes even mundane activities into heroic feats. His personal recommendation is *Scissor Seven*, a lesser known but hilarious and heartfelt Chinese anime on Netflix.

Even with his growing success, Kenneth remains humble. He attributes much of his wisdom to being observant—watching others succeed and fail and learning from both. He's quick to emphasize that he doesn't want to build the next Google; he wants sustainable, high-quality impact. That's why ECA limits cohorts to just twenty students per class to ensure personalized attention and growth.

When asked about claims that SIEM and SOAR are "dead technologies," Kenneth doesn't flinch. "They've been saying that since I was in college. I'm still waiting." He explains that these tools are foundational—they aggregate, automate, and streamline threat detection and response. What's failing isn't the technology; it's the misalignment between organizational maturity and the tools they purchase.

"You can't buy a pool if your house doesn't have walls," he says. In other words, companies need to mature before implementing complex solutions. Kenneth's ability to articulate this kind of industry wisdom with clarity and humor sets him apart.

He knows where he thrives and where he doesn't, delegating tasks like accounting and marketing and trusting specialists to manage those aspects of the business. His energy is focused on what only he can do: strategic vision, technical leadership, and community building. He surrounds himself with advisers and coaches, always looking to learn and grow.

He doesn't shy away from hard truths, either. Not every student will make it. Not everyone is ready to invest in themselves. But those who do? He goes to bat for them, introducing them to hiring managers, helping them network, and preparing them to be both technically capable and personally compelling.

Whether he's teaching, bidding on contracts, or discussing anime villains, Kenneth Ellington embodies the fusion of discipline, humility, and Black excellence. He's part of a growing movement of technologists and entrepreneurs of color who are rewriting what success looks like in cybersecurity, and he's just getting started.

As Kenneth says, "If you get knocked down—whether by a missed contract, a sparring partner, or life—you get back up. That's what makes you successful."

A Moment of Reflection:

1. **Kenneth pivoted into cybersecurity after starting his career in a different field.**

    What is stopping you from making a similar shift? What limiting beliefs do you need to challenge to take your next step confidently?

2. **He created Ellington Cyber Academy not just to educate, but to uplift others through accessible, practical training.**

    What unique knowledge or experience could you package into a resource or tool to help someone else get started?

3. **He stressed the importance of foundational knowledge before certifications.**

    Are you rushing to collect certifications without understanding the basics? What foundational concepts do you need to spend more time mastering?

4. **Kenneth emphasized consistency over speed—progressing every day through deliberate effort.**

    What does consistent daily action look like for you? Can you dedicate even thirty minutes a day to your cybersecurity growth?

5. **He's a champion of representation, creating space for others who don't see themselves in the industry.**

    How does seeing someone who looks like you in cybersecurity affect your confidence? What kind of representation do you hope to provide one day?

Dr. Joseph, Daryl, and Kenneth are powerful examples of what leadership from the front looks like. In the absence of direction, they created paths. In the face of obstacles, they kept showing up.

They are the blueprint.

Each one of them is grinding, building, mentoring, speaking, and stretching the limits of what's possible in cybersecurity. Whether it's running a community study hall, mentoring other veterans, launching a podcast to amplify Black excellence, or simply showing up in rooms where few of us are seen—these individuals are blazing trails and lighting the way for others.

We're not just watching history; we're building a legacy. And that legacy starts with each of us choosing to lead in whatever way we can.

CHAPTER 2

Mentorship as a Movement

Mentorship is both a gift and a commitment. Not everyone has the skill, and even fewer have the desire to carry it out. But for some, mentorship isn't just a role; it's a calling. Every guest featured on the "Ask a CISSP" segment of *The Other Side of the Firewall* answered that call with grace, knowledge, and humility. For this chapter, I want to shine a spotlight on three people who took that calling and elevated it into a mission: Matthew Hale, Professor Roger Whyte, and Rico Randall.

These brothers represent the highest standard of what it means to educate, empower, and lead in cybersecurity. The kind of people who talk about change and embody the change. In the military, we had a word for folks like this: the epitome. The real McCoy. The ones who live by the standard, then challenge it to rise higher. What follows are the stories of these three exceptional men—how they teach, how they lead, and how they're building a future where cybersecurity professionals know their history and are ready to make history.

Matthew Hale

Ask A CISSP | Meet Matthew Hale - Author and CEO of We Gonna Learn Today

How Matthew Hale is Revolutionizing Black History Education Through Technology V2

Matthew Hale's journey is a masterclass in reinvention, intentional legacy building, and using tech to preserve culture. A retired, disabled Marine veteran with a background in computer science and engineering, Hale took everything he learned from a twenty-year military career—including stints in advanced tech programs like the V-22 Osprey and Marine Special Operations Forces. He funneled it into a labor of love called WeGonnaLearnToday.org, the largest digital interactive Black history website in the world.

When most people retire, they rest. But Hale doubled down. It started as a passion project to educate his grandkids about their history, then became a ten-book activity workbook series—each filled with puzzles, quizzes, and educational narratives. He didn't stop there. Leveraging his expertise in Azure, VMware, and Red Hat systems, he built an entire interactive learning platform from scratch. The site covers everything from Black inventors and entrepreneurs to cultural icons and unsung heroes, allowing users—children and adults alike—to experience Black history through games, animation, and storytelling.

This isn't just a history lesson. It's an ecosystem of empowerment. Hale's platform introduces learners to over 550 historical and contemporary Black figures, organized by subject area and enhanced by music, games, and downloadable workbooks. It's representation with intention. It's pedagogy with power. And most importantly, it's Black history made interactive, accessible, and engaging.

What makes his work unique is his commitment to showing how we've always been part of the narrative, even when history books leave us out. He's turned libraries, archives, and patents into living, breathing stories. Hale reminds us that Black contributions to America aren't footnotes. They are the foundation.

He's done it all while keeping the content free, because knowledge, especially the kind designed to heal and uplift, shouldn't come with a paywall. He even built a road map for future content drops, ensuring that every month the platform grows, just like the legacy it represents.

Hale's methodology is community-informed and research-rich. He started by asking his network who they wanted to learn more about. And when few responded, he dug in anyway. He unearthed legends and pioneers who broke barriers in tech, politics, music, art, and sports. From Moms Mabley to Carter G. Woodson to Shaka Zulu, the site spans continents and centuries. It's a celebration and reclamation all rolled into one.

Today, Hale speaks at schools, appears on local news, and collaborates with educators and nonprofits to get his platform into classrooms nationwide. In 2025, he plans to launch civics and financial literacy modules to ensure young people learn where they come from and how to navigate where they're going. He's also adding Spanish-language features and tiered learning by age group, proving that Black history is for everybody, every day, and not just in February.

His advice to the community? Don't just learn—engage. Use the site to fill in the gaps that school systems won't. And don't wait until adulthood to understand how credit, APR, and compound interest work. Teach it now, while they're still dreaming.

When he's not building digital legacies, Hale unwinds with video games, basketball, music production, and family. His passion for culture isn't limited to the classroom; it flows through everything he creates. He raps, produces beats, and even builds educational games where students learn about Black icons while playing Frogger or solving crosswords.

Matthew Hale proves that you don't need a big budget to create big change. You just need vision, consistency, and love for your people. He's not waiting for history to catch up; he's making sure we never fall behind.

A Moment of Reflection:

1. **In what ways does Matthew Hale's military background influence his leadership style and his approach to cybersecurity?**

   Reflect on how structure, discipline, or chain of command show up in his insights—and how that experience intersects with being a Black man in tech or the military-industrial complex.

2. **How does Hale balance professionalism with authenticity, especially when representing his identity as a Black man in a predominantly white, male-dominated field?**

   Consider how he speaks about code-switching, representation, and what it means to "bring your whole self" to work.

3. **What does Matthew Hale's journey tell us about the systemic barriers Black professionals face in tech and security fields?**

   Look at the subtle and explicit challenges he describes—networking, mentorship access, or being underestimated.

4. **How does community support or cultural identity show up in Hale's career narrative, and why is it important in spaces like cybersecurity?**

   Think about how the importance of communal values, giving back, or lifting as you climb is embedded in his reflections.

5. **What can emerging Black professionals learn from Hale's story about resilience, purpose, and the importance of owning your narrative?**

Reflect on the power of storytelling, legacy, and visibility in creating more equitable professional spaces.

Professor Roger Whyte

Teaching and Sharing Expertise Ft. Professor Roger Whyte's Passion Season 2

Roger Whyte wasn't born a technologist. He became one when boredom in finance pushed him into curiosity. With an MBA in accounting and a job at PricewaterhouseCoopers, Roger understood that corporate prestige didn't feed the soul. "I didn't want to wake up in the morning," he recalls. "That's the worst feeling in the world."

His second act came through a tech school and a help desk role at NASDAQ. It wasn't glamorous. In fact, it was chaotic, loud, and sometimes brutal, especially when trading systems crashed, and brokers screamed over lost millions. But Roger loved it. "They cursed us out every day. But it taught me troubleshooting, people skills, and how to operate in a crisis."

That experience became the foundation for a career that led him to become a senior cybersecurity architect and virtual CISO, advising high-stakes clients on digital infrastructure and security policy. But Roger never forgot who he was, where he came from, or who wasn't getting access.

He looked around his corporate team one day and realized he was the only Black person among hundreds. That moment changed everything.

He launched a mission: get ten thousand Black people into cybersecurity. Not only trained but hired. Not only certified but confident. That mission became the Professor Roger Cyber Lounge, a chill-but-serious space where people could ask questions without fear, build real skills, and be seen.

He's trained over five thousand people so far, from truck drivers to nail techs to retail employees, and plans to stick with them for years, helping them go from level 0 to level 3 and into management. "I want them to make six figures," he says. "Financial stability is part of freedom."

Roger doesn't just teach A+ or Security+. He teaches how to write a corporate email, survive a passive-aggressive meeting, and navigate an industry that often wasn't built for us. He's not a cheerleader; he's a strategist. And he builds people, not pipelines.

Even now, he's expanding into AI education. He sees what's coming. "If I learn AI and nobody else does, they have to hire me." It's that clarity and hustle that makes Roger a cyber pro and a cultural anchor.

His students get jobs, dignity, direction, and a mentor who sees them.

Roger's story is about more than breaking into cyber. It's about rewriting the terms of entry. Because when you've already helped five thousand people get in, you stop knocking on doors.

You start building your own buildings.

A Moment of Reflection:

1. What does Roger Whyte's shift from finance to cybersecurity reveal about the difference between success and fulfillment—especially for Black professionals navigating white corporate spaces?

   Reflect on the emotional and psychological toll of fitting into systems that weren't designed with Black well-being in mind.

2. Why is Roger's approach to cybersecurity training—focusing on dignity, cultural intelligence, and survival skills—so impactful for people entering tech from nontraditional backgrounds?

   Consider how his model counters traditional, often elitist, gatekeeping in the tech industry.

3. How does Roger's realization that he was the "only one" in the room shape his mission, and what does it say about the urgency of representation in cybersecurity and beyond?

   Think about the emotional weight of isolation in predominantly white spaces and how that can spark revolutionary change.

4. Why are financial literacy and stability framed as part of freedom in Roger's mission—and how does this connect to broader historical and systemic issues facing Black communities?

   Consider the legacy of economic exclusion, from redlining to tech disparities, and how building generational wealth becomes a form of resistance.

36

5. **What does Roger Whyte's story teach us about redefining leadership in tech spaces—from being the "only one" to becoming the one who creates opportunities for thousands?**

   Reflect on how he models servant leadership, community-centered innovation, and the power of cultural vision in reshaping industries.

Rico Randall

Building Community, Diversity in Cybersecurity, and the Importance of Soft Skills Season 2

Long before he became a senior consultant at Red Hat or inspired thousands through the *DEM tech folks* podcast, Rico Randall laid optical cable through war zones. A tactical data network administrator in the Marine Corps, Rico spent eight years stationed everywhere from Okinawa to North Carolina to Central Command in Tampa—places that would form the blueprint of both his technical knowledge and his people-first leadership.

His transition out of the military wasn't driven by fear—it was engineered with precision. With the support of a retired superior and a plan sharpened by ambition, Rico dove into certifications. While others warned it would take over a year to pass the CISSP, Rico cleared it in three months. No boot camp, just hustle. "Shon Harris's All-in-One, Boson audio, and a whole lot of grind," he says.

The real game-changer wasn't only the cert; it was community. Rico leaned on his network, sharpened his Linux acumen when VMware passed on him, and joined spaces like Women in Linux, where mentorship was the currency. Eventually, that same community pushed him to apply at Red Hat. He wasn't sure if this company would see his worth. They did. Now he's helping secure global systems with OpenShift and Kubernetes while mentoring future technologists every step of the way.

But ask Rico what he's proud of and the answer won't be Red Hat. It won't be the podcast, where he interviews cyber pros from cruise ship busboys to NASA interns. It's legacy.

Rico teaches binary to eight-year-olds at his local Boys & Girls Club. He breaks tech down until it sticks, driven by a simple belief: "Every kid should be our kid." The dream isn't only to lead in cybersecurity. The dream is to light a spark in someone else that leads them to do the same.

He calls it "building the wall," brick by brick. A wall made of soft skills, certification, and confidence. Then he opens the door. "Mentorship is where you find the path," he says. "Coaching helps you walk it. Advocacy? That's when someone opens the door for you when you're not in the room."

It's this combination—technical depth and community conviction—that makes Rico's story a blueprint for the future of cybersecurity. Whether you're a transitioning veteran, a career switcher, or someone looking for their way in, Rico reminds us: you don't have to come from the perfect place; you just have to start where you are.

A Moment of Reflection:

1. **Rico transitioned into cybersecurity after serving in the military, bringing with him leadership, structure, and discipline.**

   How are you leveraging your past life experiences—even if they're nontechnical—as strengths for your cybersecurity journey?

2. **He emphasized the importance of finding mentors and not being afraid to ask questions.**

   Who are your current mentors? If you don't have any, who in your network or extended circles could you reach out to today?

3. **Rico shared how his first exposure to cyber came from doing the job without even realizing it had a name.**

   Have you ever been "doing cybersecurity" without the title? What skills have you already developed that you can now put a name to and build upon?

4. **He highlighted the significance of community and giving back to those just starting.**

   In what ways can you create or contribute to a learning space for others, especially those from underrepresented backgrounds?

5. **Rico's humility and hunger to keep learning—even with success—stood out.**

   How do you stay grounded while leveling up? What keeps your motivation steady even when the recognition or reward doesn't come right away?

Matthew, Roger, and Rico answered the call, and they became the call. Their paths prove that mentorship, when rooted in purpose and cultural awareness, becomes a powerful force for transformation. Each of them is building bridges across generations, making sure that the next wave of cybersecurity professionals is technically sound and deeply grounded in community, history, and excellence.

Their legacy is already taking shape—not just in certifications earned or job titles held, but in lives changed and doors opened. As you reflect on their stories, remember mentorship isn't always loud, but it echoes across time. And for those walking the path behind them, that echo is a compass pointing toward greatness.

CHAPTER 3

Cultivating Community for Cultural Belonging

For Rebekah Skeete, Yvonne Rivera, and Jai Salters, building community isn't optional; it's essential. Community is where belonging begins. It brings like-minded people together across lines of origin, culture, and heritage. Whether it's rooted in shared experiences or a common vision for the future, gathering with kindred spirits gives us the space to learn, to teach, and most importantly, to empower one another.

42

These three trailblazers recognized that truth and took decisive action to establish vast, purposeful communities for those frequently marginalized. What they've built is powerful and necessary.

Rebekah Skeete

Building Technical Skills and Community Ft. Rebekah Skeete, COO, BlackGirlsHack Season 2

Rebekah Skeete didn't set out to become the COO of a national cybersecurity nonprofit. In fact, when she first joined BlackGirlsHack (BGH), she was searching for a place to grow, learn, and not feel alone in tech. But she found more than community; she found a calling. Today, she's one of the core leaders behind a movement that's helping thousands of Black women and girls break into cybersecurity, stay there, and thrive in the space.

She doesn't talk like an executive. She talks like a builder—clear, honest, and a little self-deprecating. "We're just a band of merry misfits," she jokes. "But we're serious about the mission." That mission? Demystifying cybersecurity and making sure it's accessible, inclusive, and real. Rebekah's kind of leadership isn't polished or performative; it's process-oriented and people-first. While other orgs are chasing visibility, she's busy running the systems that make that visibility sustainable.

Rebekah began her role as COO in 2021 but had the opportunity to step in as interim executive director at a crucial moment. Founder Tennisha Martin had undergone surgery and needed time to recover. Rebekah didn't hesitate. She took over the day-to-day operations: coordinating partnerships, managing programs, handling logistics, and making sure the community kept running. Behind the scenes, she discovered a labor of love that most people never see. It's easy to assume that nonprofits just happen, that programs appear. But everything at

BlackGirlsHack—every cohort, scholarship, book club, and conference—is the result of invisible labor. And Rebekah took it on, not because it was easy, but because it mattered.

She's not the face of the organization, but she's the engine. And she likes it that way. Her work is powerful: balancing her full-time role as a security engineer, managing the backend of a national nonprofit, and still finding time to show up for members on Discord, on Zoom, and in real life.

Ask her what she's proud of and she'll probably mention SquadCon, a cybersecurity conference created by BlackGirlsHack with intention and inclusion at its core. No gatekeeping. No assumptions. Just access, authenticity, and unapologetic joy. SquadCon wasn't about chasing clout—it was about building something real. She still lights up when she talks about the Lyft driver who donated five dollars and inspired her to waive his entry fee. "That five dollars meant something," she says. "It meant he believed in us."

That belief is what fuels her. It's what keeps her running cohorts that helps members earn certifications in red teaming, blue teaming, and now artificial intelligence. It's what keeps her leading book clubs that start with cyber texts and often evolve into mental health check-ins. It's what keeps her in fitness competitions with other BGH members, some of whom are older and consistently outrun her on the Nike Run Club app. They roast her lovingly, and she laughs and keeps going.

There's a softness in how she leads, but don't mistake it for weakness. Rebekah is strategic. She understands systems—how to build them, how to fix them, and how to protect the people inside them. She understands that cybersecurity isn't just a career path but a survival tool.

And she knows that being visible, vocal, and vulnerable are all radical acts in a space that still sidelines Black women.

She often says the name BlackGirlsHack is like a bat signal. It's how she found the community. It's how others find their way, too. "It tells people: you're not the only one. You're not too late. You're not too weird. You're not too soft. You're right on time."

That's the kind of leadership Rebekah Skeete brings into every room, whether it's a conference hall or a Discord channel. She leads from behind, besides, and sometimes right in the middle of the mess, holding it all together with empathy, spreadsheets, and stubborn optimism.

She's not interested in being famous. She's interested in building something that lasts. And in a field that often rewards ego and exclusion, she's building a legacy out of care, process, and people.

If you're looking for a blueprint for community-led cybersecurity, don't look for perfection. Look for the misfits. The ones like Rebekah, who chose to build something better.

A Moment of Reflection:

1. How does Rebekah Skeete's leadership challenge traditional definitions of power and success in the tech and nonprofit world—especially for Black women?

   Reflect on the difference between visibility and impact, and how Rebekah reclaims power by leading with empathy, community, and process.

2. What does the phrase "a band of merry misfits" reveal about how BlackGirlsHack sees itself—and why is that identity important in reshaping who belongs in cybersecurity?

   Consider how this language disrupts elitist, exclusionary narratives in tech and embraces authenticity, imperfection, and joy.

3. Why is Rebekah's behind-the-scenes labor—what some might call "invisible work"—so critical to the success of BlackGirlsHack, and how does this reflect broader patterns of underrecognized labor among Black women in leadership?

   Think about the historical burden of care, emotional labor, and logistics that Black women often shoulder in movements, organizations, and families.

4. How does Rebekah's story highlight the role of community in not just entering cybersecurity but surviving and thriving within it?

   Explore the importance of mentorship, mental health check-ins, fitness challenges, and book clubs as holistic support systems.

47

5. **What can we learn from Rebekah's focus on systems-building—rather than personal branding or clout-chasing—about what it takes to build lasting, liberatory institutions in tech?**

    Reflect on how she is building legacy over likes and why that is relevant for future generations of Black technologists.

Yvonne Rivera

Ask A CISSP | Meet Yvonne Rivera - CEO, CISO, and Co-Founder of CyberMyte Season 2

Yvonne Rivera joined the military at seventeen, unsure of what an IT specialist even was. She just knew she would rather not climb poles. She signed up for the unknown and discovered a life in cybersecurity—one that would take her from laying cable in war zones to leading her own secure cloud company as a CEO, founder, and force for access in tech.

Her earliest days didn't involve pristine labs or corporate security suites. They involved crawling through ceilings in palace ruins in Iraq and laying fiber for internet access in university buildings and women's learning centers. Her antivirus came on a CD. Her patching was done by hand. And the machines she secured were dusty, unstable, and scattered across conflict zones. "We were just patching Exchange Servers in war zones," she remembers. "That was cybersecurity back then."

After three deployments, Yvonne came home with more than discipline; she came back with perspective. She transitioned into civilian roles, eventually managing risk and compliance for government hospitals. She built cyber programs from scratch, literally writing out SOPs by hand, training staff, and pushing back against outdated policy. When she was told she couldn't test systems because of ID badge requirements, she asked, "Are we trying to keep the network safe or just check a box?"

That's been her question ever since.

She spent years watching brilliant small businesses get denied access to federal contracts—not because their solutions didn't work, but because they couldn't afford or navigate the compliance maze of frameworks like RMF, FedRAMP, or CMMC. So, she did what she had always done: create a solution. CyberMyte, her company, was built on the belief that innovation shouldn't be blocked by bureaucracy. Using 80 percent open-source tools, she offers secure, affordable, cloud-native services that help small businesses get compliant—and get in the game.

But Yvonne isn't just a CEO. She's a mother of five. A trauma survivor. A fourth-generation Army veteran. And the deputy executive director of Raíces Cyber Org, where she mentors and empowers Latinx professionals across the cybersecurity pipeline. Her work is technical and transformative. She builds bridges for people who never thought they belonged in tech, scaffolding systems that allow healing and hope to live alongside code.

She talks about inclusion in terms of access—who's invited and who's able to thrive once they arrive. That's why she builds tools for K–12 education, so kids can start early. That's why she mentors young professionals who are trying to break into cybersecurity without degrees or connections. That's why she sponsors Minecraft memorial servers for children of fallen veterans, helping them grieve in a digital world built with care.

For Yvonne, cybersecurity isn't abstract. It's survival. It's dignity. It's the ability to protect data, and dreams. She still remembers sitting in community meetings where brilliant founders couldn't land contracts because they didn't have a checklist. She remembers trying to build trust in systems that weren't designed with her—or her community—in mind. And she remembers what it felt like to be underestimated. She doesn't want anyone else to feel that.

So now she teaches. Builds. Mentors. Advocates. She runs her company with the kind of precision that only military training can provide, but she leads her teams with heart. She isn't interested in empty DEI metrics or shallow visibility. She's interested in systems that last, in platforms that promote healing, and in architecture that makes room.

There's nothing flashy about the way Yvonne leads. But there is a fire. A quiet, unshakable fire that says: "We belong here. And we're not going anywhere."

A Moment of Reflection:

1. How did Yvonne's experience as a young soldier laying cable in war zones shape her understanding of cybersecurity as more than a career—but as a tool for survival and justice?

   Think about how lived experience in conflict and service gives her a different lens than many traditional cyber leaders. What does that add to the conversation around national security and community care?

2. Yvonne challenges bureaucratic systems that block access for small businesses and marginalized communities. What does her work reveal about the intersection of policy, power, and equity in cybersecurity?

   Reflect on how frameworks like RMF or FedRAMP can both protect systems and unintentionally gatekeep innovation—and how she's working to change that.

3. Why is it significant that Yvonne leads with both technical expertise and personal vulnerability—as a mother, trauma survivor, and Latina leader?

   Explore how her multidimensional identity challenges the "neutrality" of tech spaces and why representation with depth, not just diversity, matters.

4. Yvonne says, "Are we trying to keep the network safe or just check a box?" What does this question reveal about the dangers of performative cybersecurity—and how does it mirror conversations about performative DEI?

Consider how her push for real-world security (and real-world inclusion) calls out systems that value appearances over outcomes.

5. **How does Yvonne's focus on community—like mentoring Latinx professionals, supporting children of fallen veterans, and building tools for K–12—redefine what a "tech CEO" can look like?**

    Reflect on how she's reshaping leadership not as a title, but as a responsibility to build systems that care for the next generation.

Jai Salters

Ask A CISSP | Meet Jai Salters - Ask A CISSP Season 2 Episode 6

In a world where entry into tech—particularly cybersecurity—is often gated by access, pedigree, and privilege, Jai Salters is building something different. Through his life's work, he is redefining what belonging looks like in an industry that rarely reflects the people it claims to serve.

Jai's journey starts with his enlistment in the US Navy, not because of a love for tech but because he couldn't afford college. Like many first-generation professionals and veterans of color, his entry point was survival. Yet through discipline, mentorship, and a relentless pursuit of growth, he transformed his path into one of service-driven leadership. Rising to become a cryptologic warfare officer, Jai combined his military precision with a visionary community mindset to found Act Now Education, a nonprofit created to democratize access to high-demand certifications and career resources for military-affiliated communities.

But Jai's impact goes beyond programming and certifications.

He is cultivating cultural belonging in a sector that historically erases the nuances of race, military service, and community ties. With over 65,000 members in the Act Now Education Facebook group, his work addresses what institutions often miss: career mobility without cultural safety leads to burnout and isolation, especially for Black and brown professionals. Jai's work centers on whole-person development—offering technical training, mentorship, résumé support, interview prep, and even professional attire for transitioning veterans.

This is an infrastructure for belonging.

He doesn't simply want people to break into cybersecurity, he wants them to see themselves in it. That means creating spaces where Black veterans, military spouses, and transitioning service members feel seen, valued, and equipped to enter the room and own it.

His goal to place a thousand military-affiliated individuals into tech roles by 2026 is more than a number—it's a moral commitment to building a future where Black and brown communities are not just included but central to innovation and security. His leadership style embodies the very theme of this chapter: cultivating community not as an afterthought, but as a core mechanism of power.

Jai also coaches entrepreneurs, particularly those from underserved communities, helping them scale not just their businesses but their belief in what's possible. He reminds us that community building is not soft work. It's strategic. It's structured. And when done with care and clarity, it is revolutionary.

Through his volunteer-led model, Jai shows that systems can be built without exploitation. That mentorship can replace gatekeeping. That knowledge, when freely shared, becomes currency. We achieve cultural belonging in cybersecurity not through diversity statements, but through daily, deliberate design.

Jai's story is not a detour—it is the map.

He embodies what it means to lead with legacy, turning his transition out of the military into a collective ascent. And in doing so, he offers us a new framework for tech spaces—one that is not only inclusive but intentionally Black, culturally grounded, and radically community-driven.

A Moment of Reflection:

1. Jai Salters emphasizes purpose over profit. How does this mindset challenge traditional views of success, and why is it especially powerful for those transitioning from military to civilian life?

   Reflect on how service, legacy, and internal motivation can drive sustainable impact, particularly within marginalized communities.

2. What role does mentorship play in Jai's journey—and how can mentorship be a tool for breaking systemic barriers in cybersecurity and tech?

   Think about the significance of community-based leadership in shaping equitable access to education and employment.

3. Jai talks about being in your business vs. working on your business. What does this distinction mean, and how might it apply beyond entrepreneurship—to leadership, family life, or personal development?

   Explore how releasing control can empower others and create room for long-term growth.

4. Act Now Education provides free resources and certification pathways. How does this initiative address both digital equity and the racial opportunity gap in tech?

   Reflect on how open access to training, tools, and community can dismantle gatekeeping—especially for Black and brown veterans.

5. Jai speaks about generational knowledge instead of generational wealth. Why is this shift in language and values important in the context of Black economic and educational advancement?

    Consider how knowledge, skills, and critical thinking are legacies that can outlive capital—and help build sustainable Black futures.

Rebekah, Yvonne, and Jai remind us that cultivating community is an act of resistance, resilience, and radical love. They've shown that when you create space for people to bring their full selves—culture, struggle, and brilliance—you don't just build networks, you build movements.

Their work continues to echo through the lives they've touched and the futures they're shaping. In a world that too often demands assimilation, they've chosen authenticity. In places where exclusion was the norm, they made room for belonging. That's what true leadership looks like—and it's the kind of blueprint we need more of.

PART II: PHENOMENAL WOMEN

To be a Phenomenal Woman is to walk in power, even when the world tries to deny you space. It's to exist with purpose, confidence, and clarity in places not built for you—but needed because of you. This energy runs deep in the lives of the women featured in this chapter.

Chapter 4 highlights women navigating male-dominated industries and building community as a form of resistance and restoration. These leaders have made their presence undeniable in cybersecurity and tech, where women—especially Black and brown women—are too often overlooked. They're breaking into the industry and reshaping it through mentorship, connection, and culture.

Community, for these phenomenal women, is more than support—it's strategy. It's how they thrive, how they pull others up, and how they ensure no one walks the path alone. Their stories are a reminder that leadership rooted in cultural belonging doesn't just change systems; it transforms futures.

CHAPTER 4

Thriving in Male-Dominated Spaces

I n her timeless poem *Phenomenal Woman*, Maya Angelou boldly rejects narrow societal definitions of beauty and power. Instead, she celebrates a deep, undeniable presence rooted in self-confidence, authenticity, and inner strength. That same energy echoes in the lives and leadership of the women featured in this chapter.

I highlight three extraordinary guests—women who are not only thriving in a male-dominated industry but actively reshaping it. In cybersecurity, where women of color are still vastly underrepresented, these leaders aren't waiting for permission or space. They're claiming both, then building tables for others to join. They're more than participants in the field; they're pioneers, mentors, and trailblazers showing what it means to lead with both brilliance and boldness.

Chelsea Pierre

The Other Side of the Firewall Presents: Chelsea Pierre CEO of Blerds Leading Technology Season 1
A Day In The Life Of A Serial Entrepreneur Ft. Chelsea Pierre, Founder of Pierre's TechHeads Season 2

Chelsea Pierre's story reads like a blueprint for Black resilience, innovation, and self-empowerment in an industry where the odds are not stacked in our favor. As the founder of Blerds Leading Technology (BLT) and Pierre's TechHeads, Chelsea isn't just breaking ceilings—she's building new floors for others to rise upon. A veteran of the US Air Force and a self-proclaimed "tech nerd," Chelsea's professional evolution spans cybersecurity, public speaking, entrepreneurship, and mentorship. But more than that, her journey is a masterclass in what it means to create your own lane when the roadblocks won't move.

She entered the tech world through military training but found herself navigating more than just networks; she was maneuvering a minefield of racial and gender bias. Early in her career, she was often relegated to "domestic tasks" while her white and male colleagues took on the real technical work. Rather than internalizing the limits others placed on her, she used her downtime to train, certify, and build her skills. That foundation would later become a launchpad for her career and for a vision far bigger than herself.

When Chelsea launched BLT, she imagined a hub where Black and underrepresented technologists could access the resources she never had, such as free labs, résumé editing, business consulting, and access to venture capital. The initiative was so successful, it grew faster than she anticipated. Instead of scaling recklessly, she paused, invested in herself again, and earned a double master's degree—one in Executive MBA and the other in information systems. Her ability to step back, recalibrate, and come back stronger exemplifies what sustainable Black leadership looks like.

Then came the pivot. After being challenged by a woman at a conference to create not just pipelines but pathways to actual employment for those she trained, Chelsea launched Pierre's TechHeads—a hands-on tech repair and cybersecurity education store that hires and trains entry-level technicians. When federal contracts proved too slow and political to access, she turned to the Army & Air Force Exchange Service and opened her first location in a military mall. She leveraged that success into a scalable model, now expanding to multiple military bases across the US.

What makes Chelsea's story exceptional is her business savvy and the intention behind every move. Her work serves the market and culture. It acknowledges the barriers but refuses to be defined by them. In her words, "Pivoting doesn't mean giving up on your dream—it means finding another way to get the tools you need."

Chelsea's legacy isn't only in the companies she builds, but in the people she lifts. From military spouses to first-gen tech students, she offers a hand—not a handout—and creates real infrastructure for Black futures in STEM. Her story invites readers to interrogate their own risk tolerance, define their purpose, and dare to bet on themselves, even when the world won't.

A Moment of Reflection:

1. **What systems do you feel excluded from—and how could you build around them?**

   Think about barriers you've faced—like lack of access, bias, or gatekeeping. Some build new paths through community, content, or certifications.

2. **Who do you serve when you succeed? How can you structure your goals with community impact in mind?**

   Success can inspire others. Consider how your goals might create opportunities or visibility for your community.

3. **If pivoting isn't failure, what does it allow you to do?**

   Pivots bring new skills, fresh perspective, and resilience. Many in cyber come from nontraditional paths—yours could be your advantage.

Map Your Risk Tolerance

Instructions:

Make two columns: "What I'm Willing to Risk" and "What I Need to Protect."

Be honest, this exercise is about self-awareness, not ego.

Write your top three goals.

For each goal, ask:

What am I willing to sacrifice to get here? (Time? Sleep? Social life? Money?)

What is nonnegotiable for me? (Family time? Mental health? Ethical standards?)

Ieshea Hollins

The Other Side of the Firewall Presents: Ieshea Hollins Chief Information Security Officer (CISO) Season 1

"If you feel like you're always stuck waiting in the proverbial hallway for a door to open, perhaps it's because you're meant to be the door—the gateway to someone else's hopes and dreams."
—*Ieshea Hollins*

There's a quiet defiance in the way Ieshea Hollins tells her story. Not the kind that roars, but the kind that endures, that resists becoming what the world expects. From childhood, she had a mind built for the backend. Her father, seeing the way she instinctively explored systems, called her a "legalized hacker." Computers weren't toys in her house; they were investments. And if she was going to take them apart, she had to do it with care, curiosity, and calculation.

That early lens of learning would go on to define her career. Hollins is now the founder and CEO of Direnzic Technology, a cybersecurity and digital forensics firm born in Monroe, Louisiana, and now operating across the US and overseas. But her story is not only about business growth. It's about vision, service, and the burden—and blessing—of being one of the first.

She began her tech journey formally studying computer science but shifted to information systems. "I could program," she explains, "but you couldn't put me in a corner coding all day. I needed to talk to people." That insight changed her path, away from isolation and toward integration. She found herself drawn to solving big-picture problems, often the ones others didn't even know how to articulate.

One of those moments came when she stumbled across a disturbing legal case involving a man accused of horrific crimes, protesting his innocence with no one willing—or able—to investigate his claims. Digital evidence was being interpreted with no scrutiny, no defense support, and no nuance. Hollins couldn't stop thinking about it. "Who helps someone like that? Who can actually get inside the data and understand what happened?" The question turned into a mission. She dove into digital forensics, pairing legal and technical literacy with a commitment to justice.

It wasn't long before she realized the limitations of forensics alone. "You can only respond to a crisis after it happens," she says. "What if we could prevent it?" In 2010, she made a bold move: she formally merged digital forensics with cybersecurity, building a model of proactive protection. This approach, which is common today, was revolutionary at the time, especially in the Deep South where technology firms were still rare, and Black women CEOs in tech were even rarer.

Her work expanded into healthcare, education, local government, and business identity protection—a field she innovated when a client's entire company identity was stolen. "People talk about personal identity theft," she says, "but who's looking out for business owners? For their domains, their branding, their entire digital presence?" It was another gap. So, she filled it.

Much of Hollins's work today centers around being a virtual Chief Information Security Officer, or vCISO. The title is often misunderstood, reduced to "outsourced tech support," but the reality is far deeper. Hollins builds entirely customized cybersecurity strategies for organizations that can't afford—or don't yet realize the need for—a full-time CISO. She facilitates tabletop exercises that guide leadership teams through simulated data breach and disaster scenarios, preparing them to respond effectively in real-world situations. She designs incident response frameworks, budgets, training protocols, and vendor audits. "We don't sell antivirus," she says. "We architect resilience."

Her training sessions are especially impactful. They're immersive, culturally aware, and often eye-opening. "People tell on themselves." She laughs. "They say, 'Oh, Susan keeps her password under her keyboard,' and then we start a real conversation." She uses those moments not to shame but to educate. At the end of each session, she delivers a lecture and a lessons-learned report to management, tailored to the actual culture and behaviors of their workplace.

Still, even with all her credentials, Hollins faces the constant fog of microaggression. She's been asked to restate her qualifications mid-meeting. She's been told outright, "I would never let you touch my servers." And she's seen firsthand the way gender politics intersect with race, sometimes even from other Black professionals. In one instance, she invited a Black male peer to collaborate on a pitch. As the conversation unfolded, it became clear the client was listening to her. Her guest grew uncomfortable, interjected, and slid his business card across the table. Later, in the server room, when he couldn't execute, Hollins quietly stepped in and did the work.

"You do this too?" he asked in disbelief.

"Yes," she replied. "I invited you so we could eat together."

It wasn't the first time she'd been challenged by someone she'd tried to support. And yet, she refuses to let those moments turn her bitter. "We've been indoctrinated not to trust each other," she says. "But we've got to move past that if we're ever going to build something lasting." She believes in the power of tribe—of building your circle, sharing information, and being the example you didn't have.

This commitment to community drives her beyond consulting. Hollins cofounded **N**orth **E**ast Louisian**A SEC**urity (NELASEC), a professional collective for cybersecurity leaders in Northeast Louisiana. Before the pandemic, she ran youth summer camps to introduce disadvantaged students to tech, bypassing the gatekeeping of degrees and certifications. "Some people are naturally good at this," she says. "But they're told they need a degree before they can even start. I want to change that."

She's now working on an assessment tool that helps people figure out what kind of cybersecurity professional they want to be. "It's like medicine," she explains. "You've got all these specializations—surgeon, pediatrician, radiologist—but in tech, we just say 'cyber' like it's one thing. I want people to know what their lane is."

For Hollins, tech is both a tool and a test. It reveals who we are— how we respond to threats, how we prepare for the unknown, how we treat people who know more than us, or who look like they shouldn't. But most of all, it reveals opportunity.

Her story is not one of arrival, but of resistance, brilliance, and community. She doesn't wait for permission. She builds systems. And she reminds us, over and over again, that sometimes the most radical thing a Black woman can do is simply take her rightful place at the table—and invite others to do the same.

A Moment of Reflection:

1. **Do I enjoy finding flaws or building systems?**

   Reflect on whether you're more drawn to red teaming and penetration testing, where the goal is to exploit weaknesses, or whether you thrive when designing secure environments, like in cloud security or architecture roles. This distinction can guide you toward roles like Pen Tester, AppSec, or Red Teamer (flaw-finding), or toward Security Engineer, Architect, or vCISO (system-building).

2. **Would I rather document policy or break code?**

   Do you light up when interpreting frameworks like NIST or HIPAA, crafting risk strategies, and translating regulation into practice? Or do you prefer reverse engineering, fuzzing, and dissecting software for flaws? GRC, Policy Analyst, and vCISO roles align with the former; Pen Tester, AppSec, or Exploit Developer roles align with the latter.

3. **Do I want to work solo or lead a team?**

   Think about whether your energy is restored in focused, independent work or by collaboration and mentorship. Solo roles like Threat Hunter, SOC Analyst, and Malware Analyst allow deep technical focus. Leadership tracks—like Security Program Manager, IR Team Lead, or vCISO—are ideal for those who want to shape teams, drive vision, and influence culture. Where do you feel most empowered?

4. **Am I comfortable speaking to execs—or prefer hands-on fixes?**

If you enjoy translating technical risk into business terms and guiding strategy at the C-suite level, roles like vCISO, Governance Lead, or Risk Officer may be ideal. If you'd rather troubleshoot systems, investigate breaches, or run scripts, roles like Incident Responder, SOC Analyst, or AppSec Engineer may better match your passion.

5. **Do I need constant change—or long-term strategic work?**

Consider whether you prefer dynamic, fast-paced environments where every day is different—like in forensics, threat intel, or IR—or whether you're fulfilled by slowly building resilient programs over time, like in enterprise risk or governance. Rapid responders thrive in SOC, Red Team, or Threat Hunting roles. Strategists find impact in vCISO, Architect, and Policy roles. Which pace aligns with your ideal work rhythm?

Mariah Simone' Denson

Empowering the Next Generation: Mariah Simone' Denson's Journey from Gamer to Community Leader Season 2

Mariah Simone' Denson is a lifelong gamer and tech enthusiast, as well as a global force for change, equity, and community building. As the founder and president of Global Patch, a nonprofit focused on empowering BIPOC individuals through access to gaming, esports, digital production, and technology, Mariah exemplifies how culturally responsive education and purpose-driven tech spaces can foster true belonging.

Her journey began with inherited consoles from her gamer father, launching a lifelong passion that would eventually intersect with her academic and professional pursuits. Through Global Patch, Mariah develops educational and career pathways rooted in community needs—whether it's unlocking access to high-speed internet during the COVID-19 pandemic or demystifying high-tech spaces like Unreal Engine and Unity. Her work actively challenges systemic exclusion by connecting marginalized communities to tools of creation and innovation, all while ensuring their safety and dignity within digital ecosystems.

A doctoral student researching the experiences of Black and Indigenous women and girls in tech—especially within video games and esports—Mariah explores how learning and critical thinking flourish through play. She sees game engines not just as entertainment tools but as platforms for workforce development, education, and even military training. Her work reveals that the skills gained through gaming—

strategy, design, storytelling, collaboration—are transferable and often overlooked as valuable assets in other industries like media, journalism, cybersecurity, and even policy work.

But what grounds Mariah's leadership is her unwavering commitment to cultivating a sense of cultural belonging. She has worked internationally—in Japan, South Korea, and the Bahamas—developing educational programs that cross linguistic and cultural borders. These experiences enriched her understanding of how people connect, communicate, and build collective resilience. Whether organizing hack retreats in Colorado Springs, leading Unreal Engine workshops, or designing cosplay-for-profit workshops in Florida, her work uplifts and celebrates diverse identities and contributions.

Mariah also urges caution and critical engagement with emerging tech, particularly AI. Rather than shunning it, she teaches her community how to responsibly use AI as a tool, always anchored in foundational learning and cultural context. Her thoughtful approach encourages children and adults alike to embrace tech creatively, yet mindfully, with the goal of empowerment rather than dependence.

At the heart of Mariah's mission is play, both in digital spaces and real life. She emphasizes joy, mental wellness, and collective rest, carving out time for gaming, surfing, and travel, and encouraging others to do the same. Her insistence that gaming be taken seriously as a cultural and economic force is rooted in love for her community and a radical vision of liberation through joy, learning, and digital agency.

Mariah Simone' Denson is a cultural technologist, an educator, a global thinker—and most importantly, a community builder who believes that we can all belong, thrive, and lead in the worlds we help create.

A Moment of Reflection:

1. How does Mariah's use of gaming and esports as educational and workforce tools challenge traditional ideas of learning and career readiness in Black and Indigenous communities?

   Reflect on how play, creativity, and cultural relevance can serve as powerful entry points into tech and cybersecurity.

2. Mariah speaks about creating access to tools like Unreal Engine and Unity for communities that are often left out of tech. What does her work reveal about the relationship between access, cultural safety, and belonging?

   Consider how access to technology alone isn't enough—belonging requires spaces where people feel safe, valued, and empowered.

3. In what ways does Mariah's global work (in Japan, South Korea, and the Bahamas) inform her approach to community building within digital and physical spaces?

   Explore how global Blackness and cross-cultural solidarity enrich ideas of cultural belonging and collective innovation.

4. Mariah centers joy, wellness, and play—not just productivity— in her leadership. How can these values disrupt grind culture and offer more sustainable models of community empowerment in tech?

   Reflect on how Black rest, joy, and softness are revolutionary in professional and educational environments.

5. **What does Mariah's story teach us about reframing what it means to be "cyber adjacent" or "tech literate," especially for BIPOC youth and women?**

    Think about how lived experience, creative knowledge, and nontraditional pathways into tech deserve recognition and investment.

The women you've just read about are redefining what leadership looks like in tech. They are dismantling outdated norms, challenging gender biases, and proving that excellence doesn't come with a preset mold. Every stride they make expands opportunities for the women who follow them, particularly those of color who might not have found their own representation in this arena.

Their journeys remind us that representation matters, not just symbolically but structurally. They are not only surviving in this "pseudo all-male sport" of cybersecurity, but they are also dominating it according to their own terms. Their presence is a sign that this field's future will be more inclusive, innovative, and powerful.

These are the phenomenal women Maya wrote about. And they're not done yet.

CHAPTER 5
Lift as You Climb

I n cybersecurity—as in life—success means more when it's shared. Lift as you climb isn't just a saying; it's a call to action. A mindset that says, "As I rise, I will make space for others. As I learn, I will teach. As I break through barriers, I will hold the door open."

This chapter highlights three powerful examples of that philosophy in action: Lynn Dohm, Delisha Hodo, and Kayne McGladrey. Each of them came into cybersecurity from a nontraditional path—marketing, education, and theater—and instead of letting that difference hold them back, they used it as their strength. And more importantly, they used it to create space for others.

These leaders don't just mentor, they build systems. They speak about diversity, equity, and inclusion, and they put it into policy, into practice, and into culture. Whether it's through Lynn's global work with

WiCyS, Delisha's groundbreaking HBCU+ Academy, or Kayne's push to reimagine hiring and mental wellness in tech, all three have chosen to reach back as they move forward.

Their stories remind us that allyship is not performative when it's ingrained in accountability and vision. Leadership isn't about being the smartest person in the room, rather it's about helping others find the courage to enter the room in the first place.

Lynn Dohm

Women in Cybersecurity: A Global Cyber Sisterhood Ft. Lynn Dohm, Executive Director of WiCyS Season 3

Lynn Dohm's journey is not one of typical career pivoting or accidental entry into cybersecurity. It's a conscious choice to lead systemic change in the industry. As the executive director of Women in Cybersecurity (WiCyS), Lynn supports women in cyber. She intentionally designs pathways, programs, and partnerships to ensure equity, representation, and opportunity in a sector long dominated by homogeneous voices.

Her narrative is driven by intentionality, a word she uses often and lives by. Lynn is not a technologist by training, but she brings a background in marketing and organizational leadership to one of the most urgent issues in tech: closing the gender gap and diversifying the cybersecurity workforce. Her story underscores a profound truth—you don't have to write code to write history in cybersecurity.

What sets Lynn apart is her systemic lens. She views cybersecurity not just as a professional domain, but as a collaborative ecosystem that must include academic institutions, government, private sector, nonprofits, and marginalized communities. She and her team at WiCyS strategically engage these sectors through research-backed programming, internships, job fairs, mentoring, and professional development.

One of the most powerful parts of Lynn's journey is her data-informed activism. She understands that to create real change, we must be willing to address uncomfortable truths—like the fact that women represent only 24 percent of the cybersecurity workforce globally, and that these numbers shrink even more for women of color. Through WiCyS, Lynn challenges tokenism and champions skills-based advancement, fostering authentic inclusion and empowering individuals from all backgrounds to reach their full potential based on their skills, not credentials.

She challenges hiring practices that center on pedigree rather than potential, and she calls out "culture fit" rhetoric as a tool often used to gatekeep. Lynn advocates for culture add, recognizing that diverse perspectives are not liabilities because they are essential for building resilient cybersecurity systems.

In addition, Lynn brings a radical sense of hope to this work. A hope that mentorship can transform a life. A hope that visibility can inspire a first step. A hope that breaking down barriers for one woman helps all women, especially those from historically underrepresented backgrounds.

Her story reminds us that leadership is not about titles; it's about creating space for others to thrive. And that allyship in cybersecurity holds meaning when it's driven by intention, collaboration, and compassion.

A Moment of Reflection:

1. Lynn emphasizes intentionality throughout her work. In your own professional or personal journey, where can you be more intentional about inclusion and equity?

   WiCyS builds programming around research and community needs. What are some challenges in cybersecurity that you think need more community-centered solutions?

2. Lynn critiques the idea of hiring for "culture fit." Have you experienced or witnessed this being used to exclude rather than include? How can we shift the conversation to "culture add"?

   Lynn's journey highlights nontechnical paths to making an impact in cybersecurity. How might your unique background contribute to cybersecurity— even if you're not an engineer or analyst?

3. As someone navigating or guiding others into cybersecurity, how can you use your platform to advocate for underrepresented voices in tangible, consistent ways?

Delisha Hodo

Ask A CISSP | Meet Delisha Hodo - Ask A CISSP Season 2 Episode 9

A Day In The Life Of An Assistant Director & Cybersecurity Advocate Season 2

Delisha Hodo never planned to work in cybersecurity. In fact, when she first saw the job listing for SANS Technology Institute, she had never even heard of the organization. She just had a desire to help people, and she was gifted at doing it. Her background was in psychology and education, not technology. But she clicked "Apply" anyway. That decision would change her life and, in turn, help change the industry.

Now the assistant director of advising at SANS.edu and the visionary behind the SANS HBCU+ Cyber Academy, Delisha's impact is undeniable. But it didn't start with certifications or code. It started with students. Her earliest professional roles were in mentorship. First, they were through AmeriCorps in East San Jose, where she taught and supported middle schoolers, helping them build reading and technology skills using donated Google coding kits. From there, she stepped into college access programs, working with high schoolers navigating FAFSA forms, scholarships, and the intimidating path of first-generation college success.

That blend of educational guidance and emotional intelligence would become her signature. Delisha is cyber adjacent, as she calls it— not in the server room or spinning up exploits, but helping others get there. She's the bridge. The guide. The reminder that belonging in this field doesn't have a uniform.

When Delisha joined SANS, she advanced from adviser to senior adviser to assistant director in less than three years. But her ambition wasn't about climbing the ladder; she widened the path for others. She focused on building pipelines for students who looked like her: first-generation, curious, and often underestimated.

Initially, Delisha played a key role in launching and expanding the SANS Technology Institute's Undergraduate Program. Now she is tasked with scaling the academies, outreach, and continuously championing initiatives, such as the ongoing VetSuccess for veterans, the Women's Cyber Academy in partnership with WiCyS, and the SANS Diversity Cyber Academy. Still, her proudest accomplishment is the creation of the HBCU+ Academy, a program dedicated to training juniors, seniors, graduates, and alumni from historically Black colleges and universities in elite cybersecurity practices and certifications.

Every Thursday night, her cohort of learners—career changers, military veterans, former nurses, teachers, and college students—meet with mentors who help them earn up to three GIAC certifications, some before graduation. It's not just about the résumé. It's about visibility. Community. Confidence. One of the biggest challenges Delisha works to overcome is silence: people who feel unsure, unseen, or underqualified. She knows that feeling. Which is why she answers every LinkedIn message with intention and offers resources like the *New to Cyber Field Manual* or the SANS Holiday Hack Challenge to anyone just getting started.

She builds programs, but more than that, she builds people.

Delisha often says, "Take the stairs." For her, success didn't happen overnight. It came step by intentional step. And even as she ascended professionally, she continued to mentor others at every level—often pulling in guest speakers, organizing soft skills workshops, and creating opportunities for others to lead. Mentorship, for her, is not a nice-to-have; it's the structure. Her story is a testament to what happens when someone decides that not having all the answers doesn't mean they can't take the first step anyway.

And if she has one warning, it's this: don't chase perfection. "Perfection doesn't mean anything," she says. "You just have to give your best—maybe it's 20 percent today and 80 percent tomorrow. But at the end of the week, if you gave what you had each day, that's 100 percent. That's enough."

She knows this because she's lived it. Building programs that serve thousands while managing her own growth, renovating her home, mentoring students, answering DMs, showing up on podcasts. Delisha is proof that purpose doesn't require perfection. Just consistency. Just care.

And when people ask how to enter cybersecurity without a degree in computer science or a background in IT, she tells them the truth: "Don't let your job title define your capacity. You're more than that. Unbox yourself."

Her legacy isn't in firewalls or exploits; it's in emails from students who passed their first certification because someone believed in them. It's in the Thursday night Zoom calls. It's in the way she shows up—fully, humbly, and always reaching back.

Delisha Hodo reminds us that the field of cybersecurity isn't just made stronger by the people who hack; it's made more human by the people who help others believe they can.

A Moment of Reflection:

1. **What parts of your background might be cyber adjacent?**

   You don't need to have "cybersecurity" in your job title to have relevant experience. Think about transferable skills—project management, compliance, healthcare, education, customer service, or even military logistics. These are often rich with risk management, data protection, or process improvement. Reflect on how your past roles align with GRC, training, privacy, or threat awareness—and how cyber doesn't always mean coding.

2. **When was the last time you took a leap without being 100 percent ready?**

   Cybersecurity evolves faster than perfection allows. No one feels fully "ready"— and waiting for that moment often means missing the opportunity. Think about the last time you trusted your instincts, learned on the fly, or succeeded despite uncertainty. That mindset is key in roles like SOC analyst, risk assessor, or even entrepreneur. What would happen if you treated your cyber transition the same way?

3. **What are you waiting for permission to do—and could you give yourself that permission?**

   Whether it's applying for a cert, speaking at a conference, or pivoting careers, we often wait for external validation before moving forward. But gatekeepers don't own your story—you do. Consider what step you've been delaying. Can you reframe hesitation as a signal to act? In cyber, especially for underrepresented professionals, self-permission isn't just brave—it's revolutionary.

Kayne McGladrey

Ask A CISSP | Kayne McGladrey - Ask A CISSP Season 2 Episode 8
The Evolving Role of CISO, Amazing GRC Tools, & The Proper Use of AI In Compliance Season 2

In an industry often misrepresented by pop culture and rigid gatekeeping, Kayne McGladrey is bringing a fresh, inclusive, and people-centered lens to cybersecurity. As the Field CISO at Hyperproof, a podcast host, and longtime practitioner with over twenty-five years in the game, Kayne joined *The Other Side of the Firewall* podcast's Ask a CISSP segment to drop gems on everything from representation and accessibility to mental health and professional fulfillment.

Kayne begins by challenging one of the most persistent myths in the field: the idea that cybersecurity is a space exclusively for hoodie-wearing, white male hackers hiding in basements. While humorous on the surface, this trope has long shaped hiring practices, industry culture, and media portrayals that excluded a wide range of people who could bring vital skills and perspectives to the table.

"We've been doing something wrong ... because if the way we've been communicating cybersecurity worked, we wouldn't have the lack of diversity that we have today."

Kayne offers a refreshingly honest look at his own journey, a theater major who leaned into his improv background and natural curiosity to carve a unique path into cybersecurity. He shares how his first role in the industry came not from credentials, but from a startup founder taking a chance on his willingness to learn. That hands-on experience, along with a hunger for reading and practical problem-solving, laid the foundation for what would become a lifelong and impactful career.

But Kayne's story isn't just about personal success; it's about structural critique and industry reform. He sheds light on the silent flaws in hiring systems that require entry-level applicants to have senior-level certifications or that filter out candidates through biased ATS software. Instead, he pushes for a values-driven hiring model that emphasizes aptitude, intent, and diversity of thought.

He's also keenly aware of the challenges faced by those trying to pivot into the field from nontraditional backgrounds—whether they're artists, veterans, or people from under-resourced communities. He praises the work of veterans' transition programs but asks a bigger question: "If we know this model works for veterans, how can we expand it for everyone—especially those who haven't had access to opportunity?"

At Hyperproof, Kayne is working on that vision. The company has put measurable DEI goals in place, including inclusive hiring practices, accessible remote work, and continuous DEI training. Hyperproof's product itself—their compliance automation platform—is aimed at reducing friction between compliance and security teams, making security workflows more human, collaborative, and intuitive. And through shows like Drafting Compliance and Top 5 in 5, Kayne makes cybersecurity education engaging and approachable.

Mental wellness is also a key theme in the conversation. Kayne opens up about his commitment to exercise, outdoor activities, and building community—whether through paddleboarding, snowboarding, or running a local board gaming Discord server. He highlights how important it is for cybersecurity professionals, especially those in leadership, to prioritize their mental health amid a fast-paced, high-pressure industry.

The episode wraps with an honest, hopeful conversation about change, from the need to audit AI in hiring for bias (like the new legislation in New York) to how cybersecurity can and should evolve into a more inclusive, ethical, and human-focused field.

"Cybersecurity doesn't just protect businesses—it protects people, communities, and our democracy. If we framed it that way more often, more people would want in."

Kayne's story reminds us that cybersecurity is bigger than tech. It's about protection, integrity, creativity, and people. And most of all, it's about making space—real, equitable space—for new voices at the table.

A Moment of Reflection:

1. How do stereotypes in cybersecurity influence who feels welcome or excluded in the field? How can we each challenge those narratives?

   What structural barriers (like certification costs or biased hiring systems) are limiting entry into cybersecurity, and what would a more equitable hiring pipeline look like?

2. What strengths do professionals from the arts, military, or other non-tech sectors bring to cybersecurity? How can we better recognize and support these transitions?

   What are some ways cybersecurity professionals—especially leaders—can actively support mental health, wellness, and work-life balance in their teams?

3. With AI increasingly used in hiring, how can we ensure these systems aren't replicating bias? Should companies be required to audit their algorithms for fairness?

In an industry often defined by gatekeeping and rapid change, the stories of Lynn, Delisha, and Kayne offer a different vision—one rooted in empathy, inclusion, and shared success. They show us what it means to lead with purpose and serve with integrity. And they prove that the cybersecurity field doesn't just need more technologists; it needs more bridge-builders, more mentors, more human-centered leaders.

Each of them embodies a radical belief: that you don't have to wait until you've "made it" to help someone else rise. In fact, the act of helping others is part of the making. They remind us that lifting as you climb isn't a burden—it's the blueprint.

So, whether you're just stepping into the field or guiding others through it, ask yourself: Who can I lift today? Whose story am I making space for? This is because, in the pursuit of equity and innovation, no individual should have to embark on this journey alone.

PART III: NEURODIVERGENT NAVIGATORS & MULTITASKERS

H onestly, I wasn't sure how to begin this section of the guide. How do you do justice to both the neurodivergent heroes and the multitasking go-getters redefining what excellence looks like in cybersecurity? At first glance, these two groups might seem different—but look a little deeper, and you'll see the powerful overlap. They're unconventional. Unapologetic. Resilient. And inspiring.

Whether navigating the world through a neurodiverse lens or juggling multiple lanes of success with finesse, they are building the proverbial plane mid-flight—and doing it with style, smarts, and heart. This section is a tribute to those whose brilliance doesn't always follow a traditional path but shines all the more because of it.

It's my hope that their stories inspire you, as they've inspired me. Because in this field, there's no one right way to succeed. But there are a million ways to show up as your whole self and make an impact.

CHAPTER 6

Flipping the Script on Neurodiversity

We don't talk nearly enough about neurodiversity in cybersecurity. Or better yet, we don't celebrate it enough. As Dr. Teresa Vasquez likes to say, many of our "neurospicy" colleagues are some of the most essential minds in the room. They see patterns others miss, solve problems with fresh logic, and guide complex projects to completion with an uncanny focus.

Neurodivergence isn't a limitation; it's often a leadership superpower.

In this chapter, I had the honor of speaking with three dynamic people who are thriving in cyber and challenging outdated ideas of what leadership and professionalism look like. Elizabeth Stephens, Dr. Teresa Vasquez, and Mark Christian are brilliant practitioners, yes—but also trailblazers who embrace their neurodiverse identities and use them to reframe what it means to belong, contribute, and innovate in this space.

Elizabeth Stephens

Ask A CISSP | Meet Elizabeth Stephens, CEO of DBS Cyber

How Did CrowdStrike Take Down The Internet?

Born in Memphis, Tennessee, Elizabeth Stephens's journey began at the intersection of culture, resilience, and curiosity. From a young age, her passions were shaped by two seemingly contrasting worlds: the raw rhythms of Memphis's Orange Mound neighborhood and the quiet brilliance of early computing. With a Commodore 64 as her first introduction to the digital world, Elizabeth unknowingly stepped onto a path that would eventually lead her into the cockpit of military aircraft and the high-stakes realm of cybersecurity.

Elizabeth is a living legend, a pioneering Black woman in cybersecurity, and a decorated combat aviator in the United States Marine Corps. Her journey through the Naval Academy, where she majored in English literature while excelling in thermodynamics and electrical engineering, defied expectations. "I didn't mean to go to the Naval Academy," she admits with her signature blend of humility and boldness. Yet, when asked if she'd fly for the Marine Corps, her answer was simple: "If I think I can do this ... I'm going to give it a try."

And try, she did. She became one of the first Black women to fly for the Marine Corps, piloting helicopters and tilt-rotor aircraft through combat tours in Iraq. But her true legacy lies not only in breaking barriers; it's in how she carried the ethos of service from the battlefield to the boardroom.

Neurodivergent by nature—though she doesn't lead with labels— Elizabeth frames her way of thinking as her superpower. "If I thought like everybody else, I wouldn't be able to see half the problems," she explains. Her mind, wired differently, allowed her to synthesize solutions, systems, and security risks that others missed. This distinct cognitive wiring—often misunderstood in traditional environments—has become a cornerstone of her success.

After retiring from the military, Elizabeth ventured into the private sector, landing roles in utility infrastructure before being recruited by Microsoft. The transition wasn't seamless. The cultural dissonance between the mission-driven military and the profit-driven private sector was jarring. "People would ignore my education, my experience, and my position," she reflects. "Black women in tech don't exist—they just don't." The microaggressions were subtle but cutting, like being assumed to be fresh out of college despite two master's degrees or being treated as invisible in rooms she helped lead.

Instead of retreating, Elizabeth innovated. She immersed herself in learning—cybersecurity, infrastructure, and software engineering—and rose to become a principal software engineer at Microsoft. But what distinguished her wasn't only her technical acumen. It was her unwavering sense of mission: protecting people.

That mission took form in DBS Cyber, her own company, named after her three children—Dena, Bailey, and Samson. DBS is not just a consultancy; it's a movement. Through initiatives like Cyber Kids and the development of TOVA, a PTSD-support chatbot, Elizabeth is democratizing cybersecurity and AI. She's bringing access and protection to those often excluded—single mothers, veterans, caregivers, the elderly, and children.

Elizabeth's neurodivergence is the rhythm that drives her work. Her mind doesn't take "no" as a final answer. Instead, she questions, breaks, builds, and reimagines systems, often running ahead of industries that have yet to catch up. In her words, "I don't run into fires because I like fire—I see the smoke before the fire starts."

In a world grappling with AI ethics, digital rights, and cybersecurity labor shortages, Elizabeth Stephens stands tall—part warrior, part teacher, but all leader. She's fighting for inclusion and designing the future from a lens shaped by war, wonder, and wisdom.

A Moment of Reflection:

1. **In what ways can neurodivergent thinking disrupt and improve traditional approaches to cybersecurity and tech leadership?**

   Think of strengths like hyperfocus, unique pattern recognition, or alternative problem-solving methods. Consider how traditional environments might limit these contributions—and what changes could unlock them.

2. **How does Elizabeth's military background inform her approach to mission-driven business in the private sector?**

   Reflect on transferable traits like discipline, risk awareness, leadership under pressure, or values rooted in service. Consider how these show up in business strategy or team culture.

3. **What are the consequences of ignoring diverse voices, especially Black women, in cybersecurity and AI development?**

   Think about missed perspectives in data labeling, policy, user experience, or ethical design. Consider where bias in tools or decision-making stems from lack of inclusion.

4. **How can we build more inclusive pipelines into cybersecurity that embrace nontraditional backgrounds and thinkers?**

   Look to apprenticeships, veteran retraining programs, or community-led initiatives. Reflect on how hiring, mentorship, and education models can be redesigned for access.

5. **What does it mean to create systems "for us, by us" in an industry that often prioritizes elite gatekeeping?**

   Explore ideas like community-owned platforms, peer mentorship circles, or products shaped by lived experience rather than just pedigree.

Teresa "Dr. T" Vasquez

Ask A CISSP ft. Dr. Teresa Vasquez On Overcoming Barriers In Tech, Mental Health, & Building Legacy

Dr. Teresa Vasquez, a.k.a. Dr. T, knows what it means to fall apart. But she also knows how to rebuild. Not just herself, but the systems, spaces, and tools that once shut her out. Her story is one of extraordinary resilience, built on a quiet refusal to stay small, silent, or broken.

She grew up early. By the age of four, she was helping raise others. By five, she had lost her mother. Her childhood was a blur—a battlefield, and surviving it took both brilliance and grit. She carried that survival with her for decades, through motherhood, relationships, tech jobs, graduate school, and burnout. Though she earned a doctorate and worked in tech for over twenty years, when she was laid off, none of that seemed to matter. She applied and applied. And nothing happened. "I couldn't even get an interview," she says. "It broke me."

The breaking didn't happen all at once. It came in waves: the anxiety attacks, the impostor syndrome, and the moment she found herself applying for food stamps. For a woman who had written policy, engineered systems, taught at universities, and mentored entire communities, the silence of the tech world was loud. It said, "You don't belong here." But she never stopped listening to herself.

What came next wasn't just reinvention, it was revelation. Dr. T enrolled in a coding bootcamp, not to prove anything to anyone, but to remember who she was. At the start, she masked heavily. She called it "Sasha Fierce mode"—a nod to Beyoncé's alter ego—so she could perform confidence even when she felt crushed inside. But eventually, the mask slipped. And what emerged was something more powerful than performance: it was presence.

She started live streaming. It began with code and tech talks but soon expanded to include cooking, conversation, music, and healing. Twitch became her outlet. Her daughter became her teammate. Together, they cofounded Repped In Tech, a platform for digital creators to be visible, valued, and unfiltered. They were building an audience and a table. One that welcomed the loud, the neurodivergent, the overlooked, and the brilliant.

When she couldn't find a space that felt safe, she created one. That's what Repped Flix became: a multimedia platform for underrepresented technologists and creators to show up and show out. No editing required. No code-switching. Just raw, smart, beautiful brilliance.

Dr. T's work is deeply personal, partnering with her daughter, they build together. Their family business isn't about optics—it's about legacy. It's about creating digital ecosystems where others don't have to beg to be seen.

She is unafraid to talk about pain. About trauma. About what it means to walk into a room and know you're being tolerated, not celebrated. But she also talks about joy. About healing. About finding purpose in unexpected places. "You don't have to be polished to be powerful," she often says. That's more than a mantra—it's a revolution.

As a mother, she leads by example. As a technologist, she builds with care. As a neurodivergent Black woman, she refuses to be minimized. Her platform centers authenticity, not assimilation. Visibility, not gatekeeping. Healing, not hustle.

Today, Dr. T teaches others how to code, how to stream, and how to rest. She mentors bootcamp grads, university students, single moms, and neurodivergent creators. Her live streams are spaces of affirmation and education—equal parts tutorial and testimony. She shows people how to write code and how to write their own story.

She often says, "Being a victim is the cost of being a Black woman in tech. But being victimized? That's a choice I won't accept." That's the heart of her legacy: not erasing struggle but transforming it.

Dr. T didn't need someone else's approval to start. She gave herself permission. Now she's giving that permission to others.

A Moment of Reflection:

1. **What part of your story have you been hiding—and why?**

   Reflect on moments you've downplayed to fit in or avoid judgment. What strengths or lessons might be uncovered if you shared that experience openly?

2. **How can you turn your struggle into strategy for others?**

   Consider the challenges you've faced—barriers, setbacks, or personal pivots. How might your journey become a framework, resource, or encouragement for someone else?

3. **If you could build your own "Repped In Tech," what would it stand for?**

   Think about the gaps you've seen in tech spaces—whose voices are missing, what support is lacking. What values, tools, or mission would your platform elevate?

Mark Christian

Ask A CISSP | Mark Christian's Unique Path in Cybersecurity Season 3

Mark Christian has never lived inside a straight line. As a military programmer, cybersecurity leader, woodworker, reef tank builder, home inspector, podcaster, content creator, none of these titles have separate identities. For Mark, they're all connected by a single thread: he was built to see systems. And when they break, he builds something better.

He started young, joining the Air Force at a time when being a programmer in the military meant passing a logic-based test that didn't care about your résumé. You either had the wiring or you didn't. Mark had it. And that test would launch him into six years of service that shaped everything that came after. He laid cable in combat zones, scanned Dells with antivirus on CD-ROMs, and got chewed out for plugging in a Logitech mouse with onboard memory—because in 2005, that counted as unauthorized hardware. That was his cybersecurity foundation. Every detail mattered. Nothing could be assumed. And all of it had to be logged.

When the Air Force phased out military programming, they offered him a path into security forces. Mark passed. He left the service with a bachelor's degree, discipline, and programming experience—ready to make a civilian impact. But the financial sector, where he first landed, wasn't built for innovation. It was built on legacy code, systems with eight-character file name limits, and COBOL ghosts no one wanted to wake. Mark realized, the future wasn't here. So, he went looking.

That's when he met Kayne McGladrey and found himself at Centrify, working on identity and authentication in ways that made sense to his systems-minded brain. He learned the technology and taught it, building training programs that elevated the brand, creating certification systems, and developing infrastructure that made clients return year after year. He moved from training to customer success to enterprise consulting, and eventually to leadership at a company called Silverfort, where he helped stand up entire US divisions and was told, to his face by a CEO, that he had saved the company multiple times.

They still let him go.

That moment was pivotal. Because even though Mark had given everything—110 percent, by his own accounting—the companies he gave it to rarely gave it back. He could keep pouring into broken systems that weren't built for him, or he could build his own. He chose the latter.

Today, Mark contracts on his own terms, leveraging his veteran benefits and years of experience to live divergently. He builds systems—technical, personal, creative—designed not just for function, but for healing. His home inspection initiative, Inspector Call Dad, blends empathy with precision. His woodworking brand, Mythic Masterpieces, creates functional art that tells stories. His neurodivergent platform, Living Divergent, is a manifesto in motion: a space where ADHD, autism, anxiety, and excellence all coexist—and are celebrated.

Mark has vision, but more importantly, he has plans. Five-year roadmaps that involve reef conservation, community living spaces for neurodivergent people, and TikTok exposés that pull back the curtain on surveillance capitalism and clipboard harvesting. His brain moves fast. His heart moves deeper. And every system he builds—whether a training program, a fish tank, or a cybersecurity architecture—is crafted with the same obsessive care.

He knows what it feels like to give everything to people who don't see you. He knows what it means to be neurodivergent in corporate spaces that value "fit" over function. He knows how rejection can turn into a blueprint for something freer. Something more human. Something made for those who can't color inside the lines—because they're too busy redesigning the page.

Mark Christian doesn't need a title to lead. He's already doing it. Quietly. Boldly. Divergently.

A Moment of Reflection:

1. **Mark's journey began with identifying systems in the military and evolved into designing his own in both tech and life.**

   What systems in your personal or professional life are broken—and how might you begin to rebuild them, differently or better?

2. **Despite being told by a CEO that he had "saved the company," Mark was still let go.**

   Have you ever over-delivered in a role and still been overlooked? What did that teach you about your boundaries and self-worth?

3. **Mark doesn't compartmentalize—his work in reef tanks, woodworking, and cybersecurity are all part of a whole.**

   How might your "non-career" interests inform or elevate your professional journey? What parts of yourself are you hiding that could actually be a strength?

4. **Mark embraces his ADHD, autism, and anxiety not as limitations, but as catalysts for innovation and empathy.**

   How has your neurodivergence (or your understanding of others') shaped the way you think, solve problems, or lead?

5. **Mark's life is a rejection of "fit culture" and an embrace of divergent living.**

   In what ways can you reimagine your path, not to fit in—but to create space for others like you to thrive?

Elizabeth, Dr. T, and Mark remind us that there's no one-size-fits-all brain in cybersecurity, or in life. They are reimagining what strength, focus, and leadership can look like when we stop forcing people to mask who they are and start embracing the power of cognitive diversity.

Their journeys challenge us to create spaces that don't just tolerate difference but celebrate it. Spaces that ask what can this person offer, not how can they fit in. Because the truth is, when we honor neurodiversity, we don't lower the bar; we raise the standard for innovation, empathy, and creativity across the board.

So, ask yourself: Are you building environments where neurodivergent minds can thrive? Because flipping the script doesn't just benefit the few—it elevates the entire field.

CHAPTER 7
Hustle and Flow

ustle & Flow—a gritty, genre-defying film from the early 2000s—was all about transformation, ambition, and unapologetically betting on yourself. And honestly, I couldn't think of a better title for this chapter.

In cybersecurity, some of the most impactful figures are the ones who didn't come up through the "traditional" paths. They built their own lanes. They mastered new skills. They turned their learning process into content, their content into platforms, and their platforms into movements.

Alfredzo Nash, Kevin Apolinario, and Derron King Jr. are the embodiment of hustle and flow. Each of them found a way to break into the field and leave a door wide open behind them. They're practitioners, educators, entrepreneurs, and mentors, all wrapped in one. This chapter is a salute to the self-starters. The pivoters. The folks who never waited for permission.

Alfredzo Nash

From Tinkering to Trailblazing: Alfredzo Nash - Season 3

Alfredzo Nash's story unfolds like a saga of curiosity, hustle, and transformation—rooted in the pulse of Mount Vernon, New York, and grown through the corridors of tech, resilience, and community. From the very beginning, Alfredzo's journey was fueled by exploration, sparked by moments as simple as tinkering with a broken PlayStation and decoding cheat codes on a Sega Genesis. His curiosity didn't just stop at play; it pushed into purpose. Watching his cousin reverse-engineer tech, sneaking free internet, and digging through cheat books planted the early seeds of a hacker mindset. Though back then, they just called it "tinkering."

He entered college with no blueprint, struggling with computer science coursework while working long shifts as a security guard. But Alfredzo is nothing if not adaptive. Switching his class schedule to early mornings, he clawed his GPA up to 3.2 and earned a degree in IT by 2007. From there, it was a grind through the trenches. He started on help desks, where he was the only Black man in a pit of admins, and thrown headfirst into Linux. He learned fast, not just because he had to, but because he wanted to. A tossed pack of RHEL CDs became his crucible; an eMachine loaded with Ubuntu became his proving ground.

Alfredzo's path wasn't paved in golden opportunities. It was wired together with hand-me-down machines, layoffs, and moments of homelessness. But he kept rising. In one memorable moment, he wrote a script that saved his art gallery employer thousands during an audit,

112

securing his spot and earning respect. His trajectory carried him from Bloomberg's data center trenches to Apple's Genius Bar, where his knack for networking (literally and figuratively) shone. When the store's phone switch failed, he looped in a backup config on the fly and became a legend—clapped back into the store mid-coffee break for being the one who saved operations.

It wasn't about flash. Alfredzo was—and still is—about the fundamentals. The Cyber Coffee Hour, which he cofounded with his longtime friend Dr. Joseph Burt-Miller, is an extension of his ethos: Black voices in cybersecurity must be documented, shared, and celebrated. Their show is a platform, an archive, a network, and a movement. What started as a conversation between JROTC alums became a mission to bring storytelling, mentorship, and education into cyber's often gatekept spaces.

What sets Alfredzo apart is that he's a builder—of systems, of teams, of communities. Whether he was rallying former Genius Bar colleagues into his startup crew at Datto or building QA pipelines from scratch, Alfredzo brought people with him. He didn't hoard knowledge; he spread it. He labbed it up in apartments, refurbished tossed-out machines into learning tools, and recruited people not just for talent, but for heart.

His academic path is equally unconventional: three master's degrees from Utica University, earned not out of love for school but out of a drive to be undeniably equipped for the future. As he puts it, "If you tell me no once, I want to know why. If you tell me no again, I want to know how."

And now? He's looking to solidify Cyber Coffee Hour as an information-sharing and research firm—turning a labor of love into a lasting institution. He wants to build a lab that uplifts others and preserves the culture, while mentoring those grinding through the same paths he once walked. As a voice within cybersecurity who understands struggle, strategy, and soul, Alfredzo Nash is the embodiment of what it means to be both a doer and a documentarian.

For those entering the field, his story is a manual. For those already in it, it's a mirror. For the culture, it's legacy.

A Moment of Reflection:

1. Alfredzo's early tech curiosity came from play—cheat codes, broken consoles, and free internet hacks. What early "unofficial" learning moments shaped your current passions?

   Think back to times you explored out of curiosity—tinkering with tech, modifying games, or finding creative workarounds. How did those moments spark deeper interest or skills?

2. Throughout his journey, Alfredzo faced layoffs, homelessness, and being the only Black man in tech spaces. How have moments of exclusion or adversity shaped your drive and mission?

   Reflect on challenges like being overlooked, isolated, or underestimated. What mindset, resilience, or sense of purpose did those experiences help develop?

3. Cyber Coffee Hour is more than a podcast—it's a legacy project. What's one community initiative you'd like to build or support that centers voices often left out?

   Consider causes or stories you rarely see represented. What kind of space, project, or platform could create belonging and amplify those narratives?

4. Alfredzo pursued three master's degrees not for prestige but for resilience. How do you currently measure your growth—through degrees, experience, community, or something else?

   Look at how you track progress. Is it tied to education, impact, self-discipline, or the people you uplift? What metric feels most meaningful to you right now?

5. His story is one of resourcefulness—refurbishing machines, self-labbing, and uplifting others. What resources are you currently underutilizing that could help elevate your learning or others around you?

   Think about free tools, mentors, networks, or even your own lived experience. What could you tap into more fully—for yourself and your community?

Kevin Apolinario

Ask A CISSP | Meet Kevin Apolinario - Ask A CISSP Season 2 Episode 3

Kevin Apolinario's journey into cybersecurity didn't begin in a data center; it started in the heat of a New York kitchen. With over a decade of restaurant experience and a stint in volunteer law enforcement, Kevin's path to tech was anything but traditional. What connected the dots was gaming. Late nights of Counter-Strike and Team Fortress with military veterans introduced him to the idea of IT certifications like CompTIA A+. At the time, he didn't even know what those were. He thought "A+" meant a good grade. But he took the leap, enrolled in school, and began fixing computers as a volunteer. His soft skills stood out, and when a hiring manager questioned his lack of experience, Kevin leaned into what he *did* have: customer service, work ethic, and the drive to learn. He landed his first job.

From there, he worked his way up through various IT roles—field tech, desktop support, MSPs, hedge funds—until eventually, he eyed cybersecurity. The pivot wasn't easy. He doubted himself, unsure if he had what it took. But then something clicked: he already had experience in IAM and cybersecurity-related tasks. He just needed to reframe it, reword it, and present it. Through networking, mentorship, and showing up in spaces where people were learning and building, he landed his first IAM role. Not because of a certification, but because someone believed in him and vouched for him. And because Kevin had already paid it forward, helping dozens of others break into tech through free coaching, résumé help, and LinkedIn content.

Kevin's YouTube channel, *KevTech IT Support*, was born out of frustration. When he first got started, online spaces like Reddit weren't kind; he was told to give up, mocked for his accent, and dismissed. But he didn't stop. He made videos anyway. Today, his channel has helped thousands of aspiring professionals break into tech. His teaching style is practical, empathetic, and real—because he knows what it's like to fail and come back stronger. He collaborates widely with other creators and organizations, always aiming to make tech more accessible to Black, Latinx, and other underrepresented communities.

Outside of content, Kevin is a mentor with Cyber Mentor Dojo, Rising in Cyber, Blacks In Cybersecurity, and other advocacy groups. He's currently building a new IT support course and exploring opportunities in tech education. His long-term goal is to move into leadership in cybersecurity, and to continue building a more inclusive tech landscape.

But at the heart of it all, Kevin is about community. He spent years caring for his father through dialysis, studying in hospital rooms, and failing exams along the way. But his parents believed in him. That belief kept him going, and now he's extending that same belief to the next generation. Whether he's mentoring veterans, teaching Latinx, or breaking down a concept in a YouTube tutorial, Kevin is proof that purpose, persistence, and people make all the difference.

A Moment of Reflection:

1. From the kitchen to cybersecurity, Kevin's journey highlights the power of transferable skills.

   What skills or strengths from your current (or past) work experience could be reframed to align with a cybersecurity role?

2. Kevin faced gatekeeping and online negativity early in his career.

   How do you handle criticism or rejection, and what mindset shifts might help you continue building through it?

3. Kevin's success began with curiosity sparked by gaming and volunteer work.

   What personal passions or hobbies have the potential to connect to a future in tech?

4. Mentorship plays a critical role in Kevin's career and in the communities he supports.

   Who in your network (or outside of it) could become a mentor—or who could you mentor in turn?

5. Kevin turned frustration into impact by starting *KevTech IT Support* on YouTube.

   What barriers or frustrations in your own journey could be the starting point for something transformative—like a blog, video series, or community initiative?

Derron King Jr.

Ask A CISSP | Meet Derron King Jr. - Ask A CISSP Season 2 Episode 5
Ask A CISSP | A CMMC 2.0 Clinic With Derron King Jr. Season 2 Episode 11

Derron King Jr.'s story is a bold narrative of intentional disruption—disrupting stereotypes, career norms, and the boundaries of what it means to lead in cybersecurity as a Black veteran and founder. Born and raised in Little Rock, Arkansas, Derron's introduction to technology was grassroots and homegrown, burning CDs for the family, troubleshooting household tech, and discovering that the skills he was nurturing were a spark for something much greater.

That spark caught fire in the United States Air Force. Originally pursuing a career tied to aircraft and flight, Derron's path took an unexpected and transformative turn when the military placed him in cybersecurity, an assignment that would become his calling. At first, he didn't see cybersecurity as a long-term fit. But encouragement from his wife and hands-on experience in network defense shifted his mindset. As he learned more about the field—incident response, risk management, communications security—his curiosity became confidence.

Derron thrived in the intersection of technical expertise and regulatory discipline, finding his niche in governance, risk, and compliance (GRC). His journey from Information System Security Officer to certified CMMC Registered Practitioner was marked by hard-earned certifications—CISSP, CISM, Security+, and more. He completed all of them while serving in highly structured and demanding Air Force environments. These experiences cemented his belief in the importance of mission-focused security and data integrity.

In time, Derron realized he wasn't just a technician but a visionary. That realization, supported by feedback from mentors and his wife, led to the founding of Priority Defense LLC, a cybersecurity consulting company with a clear purpose: protect Department of Defense contractors and small businesses navigating the high-stakes world of regulatory compliance. His company bridges a major gap that supports historically underrepresented professionals and companies often overlooked in federal cybersecurity contracting.

As a Black entrepreneur and founder in the federal cybersecurity space, Derron stands out for his certifications and his leadership. He's part of a small but growing group of professionals of color, carving out space in an industry where representation is still far too rare. His mission is personal: help others enter and succeed in cybersecurity, especially in domains like CMMC, that remain niche and misunderstood but are critical for national security.

Derron's work involves helping organizations prepare for and pass CMMC audits, understand scoping requirements, and evaluate external service providers—tasks that require precision, trust, and strategy. His influence extends beyond consulting; he creates tools, shares breakdowns of new federal regulations on LinkedIn, and regularly contributes his knowledge to the community. Derron believes cybersecurity is not just about protection; it's about equity, access, and empowerment.

Despite the demanding nature of his work, Derron is equally committed to balance. With a strong focus on family, he carves out dedicated time for his wife and daughter, building their relationship with intention and joy. Sundays are sacred as work stays off, and the laptop is closed. Whether it's planning all-inclusive vacations, enjoying movies, or challenging his father's favorite sports team just for fun, Derron stays grounded in what matters.

What's most striking about Derron isn't just his technical brilliance or entrepreneurial success, but it's his vision for sustainable, community-rooted leadership in cybersecurity. He's here to secure systems and help others see themselves in the field, take ownership of their futures, and protect what matters most, from their personal data to their generational wealth.

A Moment of Reflection:

1. What does Derron King Jr.'s story teach us about the importance of adaptability in shaping a successful career path, especially for Black professionals in tech?

   Think about how pivoting between roles, industries, or learning curves has shaped your own journey. How has flexibility helped you grow—especially in spaces where representation is limited?

2. How does Derron's work in GRC challenge traditional perceptions of cybersecurity, and why is it critical to include these less "flashy" roles in the conversation?

   Consider how roles in governance, risk, and compliance often go unnoticed compared to offensive or technical positions. What value do these roles add, and how might they align with your strengths?

3. What are the unique challenges and advantages of starting a business as a cybersecurity founder from a military background? How does cultural background play a role in navigating these paths?

   Reflect on how discipline, structure, or mission-first thinking from service life can influence entrepreneurship. How might culture, identity, or lived experience shape how you lead?

4. How does Derron integrate personal values—especially family, discipline, and service—into his professional life, and what lessons can be drawn from his approach to work-life balance?

Think about the personal principles that guide your professional decisions. Where could you better align your work with what matters most to you?

5. **In what ways does Derron's presence as a Black leader in federal cybersecurity reshape the landscape for future generations, and how can institutions better support this kind of leadership?**

    Consider how representation influences access, trust, and innovation. What can organizations do to elevate diverse leadership—and how can you play a part?

What Alfredzo, Kevin, and Derron have in common isn't just their success—it's their refusal to stay boxed in. They took the "hustle" mindset and married it to purpose. Each of them shows us that career-switching, content creation, and community building aren't side hustles; they're acts of leadership.

In a field that often emphasizes degrees and linear progression, these men built alternative routes, and then invited others to walk them too. That's the real flow: when your journey becomes a map for someone else.

So, the next time you think your background doesn't "fit," remember this: the game is changing. And folks like Alfredzo, Kevin, and Derron are the ones rewriting the rules.

PART IV: VETERAN TRANSITIONS

T he transition from military to civilian life is one of the most under-discussed, underestimated journeys a person can face. Whether you served for a few years or a few decades, you sacrifice time, energy, and often identity—under the vague promise that everything will fall into place once you return to "regular" life. But let's be honest: for many, it doesn't.

For some, the transition is smoother than others, but easier doesn't mean easy. I speak from experience. After twenty years in the military, I left with no debt from education or certifications and had a strong network thanks to dope assignments and the podcast. I thought I was good—certified, credentialed, and experienced. But the truth hit hard. I jumped headfirst into a tech and cyber job market in the middle of a layoff wave. Recruiters I'd built relationships with over two years suddenly disappeared. I applied to 150 roles that I was fully qualified for—and heard crickets.

Then came application 151. A retired Marine named Stephen Haley found my résumé and took a chance on me. Later, two more opportunities came—thanks to my brother from another mother, Chris Jones, who advocated for me in rooms I didn't even know existed. That's when I learned the realest lesson: It's not just about what you know; it's about who's willing to speak your name when you're not in the room.

So, if you're a veteran—or a career switcher—here's what I'll say: make friends, ask questions, and let your passion speak louder than your résumé. Show up in ways that let people see you. You never know who's listening, watching, or ready to open a door.

CHAPTER 8

Reinventing the Mission

Cybersecurity After the Military & Law Enforcement

Vets helping vets—that's the new mission. When we take off the uniform, the mission doesn't disappear. It transforms. We go from defending national interests to defending our future, our families, and our peace of mind. The transition out of military or federal service is a different kind of battlefield, one that no Transition Assistance Program can truly prepare you for.

And that's especially true for those coming out of law enforcement and federal agencies like the FBI, where identity, routine, and purpose are tied so tightly to the role. Moving from those structured, high-responsibility careers into the chaos of corporate America is jarring. Translating those skills? Even harder.

But we're not alone.

This chapter highlights three exceptional veterans of their respective fields—Jeffrey Lodick, Derrich Phillips, and Miguel Clarke—who've not only made the transition but are actively paving the way for others. They're educators, entrepreneurs, and cyber advocates redefining what it means to serve after service.

Jeffrey Lodick

Ask A CISSP | Meet Jeffrey Lodick Season 2 Episode 11

Jeff Lodick's life reads like a masterclass in transformation, intention, and service. A native of Buffalo, New York, Jeff entered the military at eighteen years old as he needed direction. What began as an escape from uncertainty became a twenty-year journey of discipline, sacrifice, and eventually, a passion for mentorship and leadership. He found his stride in the Army later in his career, around year fourteen, proving that purpose sometimes takes time to bloom.

From jumping out of planes as a jump master to guiding junior soldiers as a leader who believed in servant leadership, Jeff built a legacy in empathy, structure, and action. His belief in "working for his people" instead of them working for him marked a leadership style that valued humanity as much as strategy.

After a knee replacement and witnessing shifts in military expectations for senior leaders, Jeff transitioned on his own terms. Instead of clinging to the familiarity of the military-industrial complex, he leaped into the world of car sales—not because it was easy, but because it was different. He wanted to learn the language of business, of sales, of people. That leap would soon lead him to Red Sky, a woman-owned small business specializing in cyber strategy and operations, where he now serves as director of customer solutions.

But Jeff's story doesn't stop at his day job. His calling is broader. Through transition coaching, speaking engagements, and mentorship—especially through FourBlock—Jeff has become a lighthouse for veterans navigating the chaotic waters of civilian life. His podcast was born from the frustration of watching others struggle with military transition. His work in life and leadership coaching draws on sports analogies and personality assessments to help young athletes become leaders, not just players.

Jeff is also rooted in family. A father to four children ranging from toddlers to young adults, he describes fatherhood as his "forever title." The intentionality he now brings to parenting, especially with his younger children, reflects a man who has learned from service and self-reflection. His time is split between supporting national security initiatives and reading Spider-Man to his daughter's kindergarten class.

Even after multiple surgeries and health challenges, Jeff embraced the 75 Hard program to restore structure and discipline in his life. It wasn't about muscle; it was about mindset. That mental toughness, born from decades of leadership, pain, and purpose, continues to fuel his service to others.

Jeff Lodick is not finished. He's building a legacy—not of titles, but of impact. Whether he's helping a transitioning service member find their voice, launching a new book series aimed at youth, or walking fifty miles in a veteran charity challenge, Jeff's mission is clear: empower, educate, and elevate.

A Moment of Reflection:

1. What does it mean to lead by serving others, and how can Jeff's example of servant leadership apply to your own personal or professional life?

   Consider leaders who prioritize listening, lifting others, or creating space for growth. Think about times when service—not status—led to meaningful impact.

2. Jeff chose to explore car sales and business instead of staying within the comfort zone of defense contracting. What does this reveal about the value of stepping outside of your comfort zone?

   Reflect on moments when you chose growth over familiarity. What risks opened new skills, confidence, or clarity about your goals?

3. In what ways did Jeff's military experience both help and challenge him during his civilian transition? How does this compare to your own understanding or experience of change and reinvention?

   Think about habits, expectations, or strengths shaped by structure. What new environments tested those—and how did they help you adapt?

4. Jeff emphasizes intentionality in parenting, professional life, and self-care. What areas of your life could benefit from more intentional structure or focus?

   Consider parts of your day or week that feel reactive. Where could clearer goals, boundaries, or routines support your well-being or success?

5. **How does Jeff's continued commitment to community service, veteran mentorship, and personal growth challenge traditional notions of retirement and success?**

    Think about examples of people who stay active in purpose-driven work. What does "retirement" or "success" mean if growth and giving never stop?

Derrich Phillips

Ask A CISSP | Meet Derrich Phillips - President and Founder of Aspire Cyber

Derrich Phillips's path into cybersecurity started with a uniform, a rifle, and a sense of duty. Just two weeks after high school graduation, he entered Army basic training. During those formative years, every keystroke was encrypted, every network line mattered, and every system had to be secured under threat of real-world consequences. Derrich learned the discipline, adaptability, and systems thinking that would become the core of his identity. He wasn't just a soldier. He was a telecom operator and COMSEC custodian, managing top-secret and classified communications in high-stakes environments like Iraq and Afghanistan.

But what separated Derrich from many of his peers was what he did with that experience. While deployed, he noticed something: defense contractors doing the same job he was but earning far more, and with far fewer constraints. That planted a seed in him. When he left the Army, he returned to Iraq—not in uniform, but as a defense contractor himself. He spent years working in security operations centers, developing his cybersecurity muscle in some of the most volatile regions in the world.

Eventually, he moved into the private sector, taking roles with top-tier firms like Lockheed Martin, Hewlett-Packard, and Bank of America. But the turning point came while conducting third-party risk assessments. He discovered that small businesses were woefully unprepared for the cybersecurity challenges they faced. Worse yet, many had been burned by overpriced and underperforming consultants. They were frustrated, overwhelmed, and underserved. And that's when Derrich knew it was time to serve again.

He founded Aspire Cyber as a mission-driven consultancy grounded in clarity, trust, and military-grade precision. His focus? Helping small businesses and federal contractors navigate compliance frameworks like CMMC, HIPAA, and ISO 27001 with clarity and ease. Drawing on years of lived experience in both combat zones and corporate environments, Derrich created a company that does more than assess—Aspire Cyber guides, educates, and empowers.

His military background echoes through every aspect of his business: from the discipline of waking at five a.m. to meditate and study to the leadership values that inform his mentorship and content creation. Whether he's building a new GRC tool, training clients through EC-Council's platform, or recording YouTube shorts, Derrich approaches each mission with the same focus he brought to the battlefield: excellence, service, and impact.

Aspire Cyber is a blueprint for how veterans can transform their military skills into lasting civilian legacies. Derrich is proof that cybersecurity leadership isn't about titles or degrees; it's about grit, integrity, and the courage to lead from the front.

A Moment of Reflection:

1. How do your past experiences—whether military, corporate, or personal—shape the way you approach challenges and opportunities in your career?

   Consider how structure, adversity, or leadership roles have influenced your mindset. What habits or perspectives do you carry into new spaces?

2. Have you ever recognized a gap or unmet need, like Derrich did? What did you do—or what could you do—with that awareness?

   Think about moments when you noticed a missing resource, voice, or service. How might you take action to address it?

3. What values guide the work you perform, and how visible are those values in your daily habits, routines, or leadership style?

   Reflect on the principles that matter most to you—like integrity, service, or innovation. Are they showing up in how you work and lead?

4. Are you using your skills and knowledge to truly serve others, or are you holding back out of fear, uncertainty, or lack of direction?

   Consider whether your impact matches your potential. What would change if you led with confidence and clarity?

5. **In what ways can you transform your own expertise into a legacy that uplifts others, just as Derrich did through Aspire Cyber?**

   Think about how mentorship, education, or entrepreneurship can extend your influence. What could you build that benefits others long after you're done?

Miguel Clarke

FBI Special Agent To Cybersecurity & GRC Evangelist Ft. Miguel Clarke

Miguel Clarke's story is more than a distinguished career; it's a reflection of how identity, passion, and purpose can evolve within, and beyond, institutions that weren't always designed with people like him in mind. As a retired supervisory special agent with over twenty-three years in the FBI, Miguel carved a path few have walked, let alone as a Black man in one of the most traditionally white, rigid federal institutions. His journey, in service and innovation, is one that speaks to technical excellence, cultural resilience, and leadership in spaces where Black voices have been underrepresented.

Miguel began his FBI career in 1998, tackling violent crimes and high-stakes bank robberies, work that placed him directly in the crosshairs of danger and demanded a commitment to community safety. But beneath the badge was a self-professed "computer geek," building PCs in the nineties to game and understand how technology moved and responded. His curiosity became the foundation for his next chapter: a pioneering move into cybersecurity, long before the digital threat landscape became a household concern.

In 2000, Miguel joined the FBI's cyber squad, one of the first agents to step into a digital battlefield that most had not yet recognized. Without formal training but fueled by curiosity, discipline, and tenacity, he handled high-profile national security cyber cases, like the Joint Strike Fighter intrusion that had broad implications for national defense and global cybersecurity. Miguel's dual identity as a protector and a tech strategist flourished. His work wasn't just about stopping criminals; it was about safeguarding democracy in the digital age.

As the cyber threat landscape evolved, so did Miguel's roles—from tracking malicious code to engaging top corporations in difficult, candid conversations about risk, resilience, and readiness. His role as a cybersecurity liaison under Chatham House Rules offered CEOs and CISOs something rare: the space to ask questions without fear of reprisal or regulatory scrutiny. He was a bridge between the FBI and the private sector, as well as between fear and clarity.

Retiring in 2021, Miguel transitioned seamlessly into the private sector, joining Armor Defense as a GRC and cybersecurity evangelist. He brought technical wisdom and a philosophy that true security isn't about eliminating threats, it's about building systems, cultures, and teams that know how to respond when the inevitable happens. His advocacy centers on the idea that cybersecurity should be woven into business as integral as finance or operations.

Miguel is a gamer with a love for Final Fantasy VII, a firearms enthusiast grounded in safety and respect, and a Nikon photography aficionado who sees the world through a lens of both art and detail. His multifaceted identity defies the one-dimensional archetypes too often imposed on Black men in public service or tech. Miguel Clarke is an expert, a storyteller, an innovator, and a cultural translator in an era where cybersecurity, like justice, demands both precision and perspective.

A Moment of Reflection:

1. **How did Miguel Clarke's identity as both a protector and a technologist shape his approach to cybersecurity within the FBI and beyond?**

   Think about how dual roles—like defender and innovator—can influence decision-making, team dynamics, or how you assess risk and mission alignment.

2. **How does Miguel's work bridging the public and private sectors reflect the evolving nature of cybersecurity leadership and communication?**

   Consider how cross-sector collaboration is becoming essential. What communication or partnership skills are needed to navigate both worlds effectively?

3. **What role did curiosity and self-initiative play in Miguel's career growth, and how can these traits be cultivated in future cybersecurity professionals?**

   Reflect on times when learning on your own opened new doors. How do curiosity and proactivity shape long-term success in fast-moving fields like cyber?

4. **Have you ever underestimated the power of your unique background or identity in a professional setting? How can I start viewing it as a strength?**

   Think about ways your lived experience offers insight others may overlook. How could embracing your story add value to your work or team?

5. **Do you see yourself as a bridge between different communities, departments, or industries? If not, what's one step you can take to build those connections?**

   Consider how you might connect technical and nontechnical voices, or bring together groups that don't usually collaborate. What small move could help you become that connector?

Jeffrey, Derrich, and Miguel show us that the mission doesn't end. It's ever evolving. These brothers didn't just walk through the door; they held it open, propped it up, and invited others in. They remind us that the skills we sharpened in service—discipline, adaptability, critical thinking—are still needed, valuable, and powerful.

But beyond the tactical and technical, they also show the emotional labor of transition—the doubts, the learning curves, the grind of reinventing yourself in a world that doesn't always recognize your experience at first glance.

Their stories tell every vet this: you are *not* starting over. You're starting *again*, with more tools, more grit, and more to give than ever before.

CHAPTER 9

Serving Again

Vets Uplifting the Next Gen

Servant leadership is a buzzword in corporate spaces, but veterans know it as a way of life. To lead, you must first know how to follow, and when you've spent years learning what it means to be part of a unit, trust your team, and lead from the front, you carry that mindset long after the uniform comes off.

The men featured in this chapter—seasoned vets who've become mentors, team builders, and advocates—don't just lead with their titles. They lead with intention. They remember what it was like to be the new soldier, the new hire, or the one trying to find their way. And now, they're using decades of experience to ensure the next generation of talent survives and thrives.

This is what it looks like to serve again—not with a rifle or radio, but with wisdom, empathy, and the heart to lift others up.

Michael Ware

Ask A CISSP | Meet Michael Ware - Chief Information Officer, NC Department of Environmental Quality

Michael Ware's journey is the embodiment of purposeful transformation grounded in commitment, resilience, and the unwavering desire to uplift others. From his early days on the flight-line maintaining B-1 bombers to his current role as chief information officer for the North Carolina Department of Environmental Quality, Michael's career tells the story of a servant-leader who continually reinvents himself without losing sight of the people behind the mission.

His military service began in aircraft maintenance, where he specialized in avionics and defensive systems. Working hands-on with jamming radars and keeping high-powered machines combat-ready, Michael developed a technical foundation and mindset established in precision, responsibility, and teamwork. During this time, he earned his bachelor's degree, proving his commitment to professional growth and long-term opportunity.

As the Air Force opened pathways for enlisted members to become officers, Michael seized the moment. At the ten-year mark of his service, he commissioned as a communications officer, marking a critical pivot from the highly tactile world of aircraft maintenance to the digital battle space of military IT. While the shift came with new challenges, including the emotional distance of leaving behind a tight-knit enlisted community, it expanded his influence. He was solving problems and now leading teams through them.

145

In his final assignment with the Air Force, Michael served as director of operations at the 83rd Network Operations Squadron, overseeing mission-critical systems from Missouri to Turkey. There, he mentored airmen, navigated complex technical missions, and refined the soft skills that would become a hallmark of his leadership style.

Retiring from the military, Michael stepped into the civilian sector with courage, though with obstacles. He applied to more than seventy-five jobs, battled through disorienting interviews, and learned—through trial and error—how to translate military experience into language that civilian hiring managers could understand. A thirty-day contracting role at the North Carolina Department of Transportation became his foot in the door, and soon after, he stepped into a CIO role, eventually landing at his current position with the Department of Environmental Quality.

Throughout this journey, Michael's mission has remained constant: serve with integrity and give back. As a mentor in his workplace, he actively helps younger professionals, especially those interested in cybersecurity, find their footing. He's engaged in state-level efforts to build internship programs targeting HBCUs, neurodiverse individuals, and other underrepresented groups. He even leveraged a conversation on this podcast to advocate for the use of hashtags and inclusive language in job recruitment—small actions with big ripple effects.

Even as laws and political pressure complicate how DEI efforts are framed in the public sector, Michael continues to push forward thoughtfully. He believes in the strength of diverse teams, the importance of perspective, and the power of intentional hiring. His DEI work is practical, lived, and experienced.

A technologist at heart, Michael is also an early adopter of artificial intelligence, leveraging AI tools to make workflows more efficient and services more accessible for the people of North Carolina. But even as he explores cutting-edge solutions, he remains grounded in mentorship and legacy. Whether offering résumé guidance, advising new cyber professionals, or helping someone discover if cybersecurity is the right path for them, Michael Ware leads with heart.

His story reminds us that leadership is not about power, but about presence. Not about titles, but about trust. And that the journey doesn't end with retirement; it evolves, creating new opportunities to serve, to learn, and most of all, to lift others as you climb.

A Moment of Reflection:

1. What values or lessons from your time in the military continue to shape how you lead or serve others today?

    Consider how skills like discipline, mission-focus, or adaptability translate into your current work or relationships.

2. How do you prepare for major transitions in your career or life, and what role does mentorship play in those moments?

    Think about what helped or hindered you during past transitions and who helped you find your footing.

3. Michael shared the importance of knowing when to speak "the language" of technical versus strategic leadership. How do you navigate different communication styles depending on your audience?

    Reflect on times when tailoring your message made you more effective—or when it didn't.

4. How do you give back to your community or industry, especially in ways that help others break barriers?

    Whether through mentoring, volunteering, or advocating for equity, think about how you pay it forward.

5. What does post-military success look like for you beyond titles and paychecks?

    Michael found purpose in leadership, service, and mentorship. What does legacy mean for you?

Dr. Eric Hollis

How Can Continuous Learning Boost Your Cybersecurity Career? Dr. Eric Hollis Weighs In

Dr. Eric Todd Hollis never imagined his journey would carry him from a small town outside Beaumont, Texas, to more than fifty countries across the globe. Yet, with thirty years of distinguished service in the United States Navy and an unrelenting hunger for knowledge, he has become a force in cybersecurity and beacon in higher education and thought leadership.

His story begins in Silsbee, Texas, but his world opened wide the moment he stepped into military life. As a Navy chief and later an officer, Dr. Hollis built a reputation for innovation and reliability in communications, operating as a personal communicator for four-star generals and admirals. That role took him around the world, relying on his ability to "MacGyver" secure comms in unfamiliar spaces, from hotel rooms to war zones. He adapted to the moment, proving time and again that being calm under pressure combined with technical acumen could keep operations secure and running.

Long before cybersecurity was the term of the day, he was hands-on in what we now call cyber operations, embedded in communications, satellite technologies, and network security. As the field evolved, so did he. Driven by what he calls "an insatiable appetite for knowledge," Dr. Hollis pursued education relentlessly, earning degrees in criminology, business, and ultimately, a PhD in organizational management with a focus on IT and cybersecurity. "Education is the new currency of the

149

twenty-first century," he says, a refrain he repeats often as a mantra and call to action for the next generation.

After retiring in 2014, he transitioned into academia, where he has taught for over seven years at multiple universities. Whether he's guiding students through their first cybersecurity course or supporting doctoral candidates in their dissertation defenses, he sees himself as a mentor first, professor second. "I always believe in giving back," he explains. And his students feel it. Many return to thank him years later, having entered the field, pursued graduate education, or launched new careers thanks to his encouragement.

But Dr. Hollis didn't stop at the classroom. With the founding of Hollis Group LLC—a cybersecurity leadership consulting firm—he has created a platform for thought leadership and global influence. His services stretch from consulting and executive training to international course development. One of his most notable achievements was designing a cybersecurity course for executives for the company Udacity, which was picked up by Israel and Saudi Arabia and disseminated globally.

As a service-disabled, veteran-owned small business, Hollis Group LLC is more than a firm. It's a vision and platform designed to provide services and shift the conversation around cybersecurity and leadership. For Dr. Hollis, it's all about reach, impact, and preparation for the future. He is currently a partner with ISACA, authorized to provide CISM and CISA training globally, and a TEDx speaker whose messages on leadership, dedication, and resilience have touched audiences far and wide.

When asked about risk and what propelled him into entrepreneurship after a lifetime of structured service, he is clear: "I had always worked for someone. I wanted my own piece of the pie." The paperwork, the federal certifications, the registrations were merely logistical hurdles. What mattered most was showing other veterans and professionals that it could be done. That they, too, could become CEOs of their own vision.

Dr. Hollis believes in the power of mentorship, and his own legacy reflects that. From helping a former service member gain admission to Harvard Law to supporting young students finding their way into cyber, he sees his role as generational and transformative. He also knows that cybersecurity is not just about firewalls and breaches; it's about leadership and culture. "Cybersecurity must come from the top," he says. "If the leadership takes it seriously, the entire organization follows."

Now nearing the launch of his first podcast and his first book— one focused on cybersecurity leadership for general audiences and another as a memoir of his military life—Dr. Hollis continues to build bridges between the military, academia, and entrepreneurial worlds. His mission is clear: elevate the profession, inform the public, and inspire the next wave of leaders.

Even in his downtime, Dr. Hollis is in motion. Whether he's riding his Peloton, driving with audiobooks queued up, or mentoring students in APA formatting and dissertation strategy, his time is purposeful. "You can make money all day," he says, "but you can't get time back. So use your time and talent wisely."

Through every phase—sailor, scholar, speaker, CEO—Dr. Eric Todd Hollis has proven that leadership is not just a title; it's a legacy. And for those willing to follow their curiosity, push past their limits, and invest in others, the impact can ripple across generations.

A Moment of Reflection:

1. In what ways did Dr. Hollis's military experience prepare him for leadership roles in both academia and entrepreneurship, and how can veterans leverage their own service in similar ways?

    Reflect on the transferable skills—from discipline to adaptability—that service members often carry with them, and how these traits can build a bridge into impactful civilian leadership.

2. Dr. Hollis calls education "the new currency of the twenty-first century." How has your personal commitment to lifelong learning influenced your career or sense of purpose?

    Consider what motivates your learning journey and how it aligns with your vision for your future.

3. How does Dr. Hollis's mentorship mindset—"mentor first, professor second"—challenge traditional ideas of authority and teaching, especially in technical fields like cybersecurity?

    Think about how mentorship differs from instruction, and how that approach might be replicated in your work or academic environment.

4. Dr. Hollis faced uncertainty when stepping into entrepreneurship after a structured military career. What personal fears or doubts might you need to overcome to pursue a dream or take a leadership risk?

    Explore your own relationship with risk and structure. What would it take for you to carve your own lane, as he did?

5. Cybersecurity, according to Dr. Hollis, is not just about technology—it's about leadership and culture. How can you influence your organization or community to take cybersecurity (or any mission-critical issue) seriously from the top down?

Reflect on the connection between trust, vision, and protection in leadership— what kind of tone do you set?

Allen Westley

Ask A CISSP | Allen Westley - Ask A CISSP Season 2 Episode 13

Ask A CISSP | AI's Role in Cybersecurity and Career Evolution

Allen Westley's journey to become a leading voice in cybersecurity and digital strategy is a story of grit, service, and intentional growth. Before he stepped foot into a classified operations center or stood before a classroom as a cybersecurity professor, Allen was a young man navigating a world of labor-intensive jobs—throwing totes in warehouses, cleaning sweatshops, and reverse-engineering processes before automation was even a buzzword. The military would become the crucible in which his discipline, technical instincts, and leadership ethos were forged.

Enlisting first in the US Army as 11B Mechanized Infantry where he operated ITV, Bradley Fighting Machines, and M1 Abrams tank, Allen managed critical equipment inventories for armored vehicles deployed in high-stress environments. When he transitioned into the Air Force Reserve, he took an unexpected leap into satellite operations, which introduced him to orbital mechanics and laid the groundwork for his future in space and cyber defense. Though he began his service on the ground, Allen eventually ran operations in major mission centers like Schriever and Vandenberg, overseeing multidisciplinary teams of engineers, technicians, and analysts tasked with protecting the nation's most sensitive systems.

After leaving military service, Allen transitioned smoothly into the defense contracting world, where he has spent over fifteen years leading cyber intelligence initiatives for major organizations. Now operating at the strategic level, Allen brings clarity to complexity, balancing national security needs with emerging threats in artificial intelligence, data governance, and operational resilience. He holds a CISSP, CSM, Security+, and an MBA, and he currently works as a cyber intelligence director, developing strategy while staying grounded in the tactical realities of cybersecurity.

Outside of his day-to-day leadership, Allen has a second calling: teaching and mentorship. As an adjunct professor, he has taught cybersecurity to international students, many of whom speak English as a second language. With patience and storytelling, Allen demystifies complex concepts, making cybersecurity approachable and empowering for newcomers. He frequently reminds students and mentees alike that cybersecurity is not just about tech but rather people, purpose, and trust.

That passion for people extends into his work as a cultural competence advocate. Allen served as the chair of the Black employee resource group at L3Harris, where he led initiatives to spotlight Black professionals, expand mentorship networks, and represent employee voices directly to the company's CEO and board. His work made space for Juneteenth celebrations, cultural competency panels, and professional development sessions that created impact that lasts beyond titles or tenures. He knows that visibility matters, especially in a field where Black professionals remain underrepresented at every level.

An early adopter and lifelong learner, Allen is now pushing boundaries through his company, Cyber Explorer LLC. He uses generative AI, virtual avatars, and voice cloning to create on-demand

155

cybersecurity training content, developing full productions solo in hours, not weeks. For him, AI is not a threat; it's a tool to scale knowledge and close access gaps, especially for professionals who are new, pivoting, or underserved.

Whether mentoring a young professional on suit etiquette at a NSBE conference, guiding a sixty-one-year-old career changer into GRC, or serving on AI and cybersecurity panels, Allen brings the same energy: approachable, prepared, and always giving back. He believes that legacy is about elevation. And every time he teaches, writes, leads, or speaks, he brings others with him.

Allen Westley isn't just navigating the digital future; he's shaping it, with the steadiness of a soldier, the mind of a strategist, and the heart of a teacher.

A Moment of Reflection:

1. **How have your past experiences prepared you for leadership or innovation in tech?**

   Think about early exposure to structure, problem-solving, or teamwork—from military, retail, education, or anywhere else. These foundations often translate into strategic thinking and resilience in cybersecurity.

2. **How can you help create more inclusive pathways into cybersecurity and AI?**

   Consider the impact of mentorship, representation, and culturally aware leadership. Even small efforts—like peer coaching or advocacy—can shift access and belonging.

3. **What does Allen's nontraditional path teach you about career growth in tech?**

   His pivot from military roles into advanced technical work shows how self-learning, curiosity, and persistence can outweigh formal credentials in a fast-moving industry.

4. **How might you use AI tools to educate or empower others?**

   Explore creative uses—like building avatars, interactive content, or mentorship bots—that go beyond productivity and help make learning more engaging and accessible.

5. **What would inclusive, constellation-style leadership look like in your work?**

This model emphasizes shared influence over rigid hierarchy. Consider how distributed leadership can support innovation, trust, and collaboration across diverse teams.

What these leaders have in common isn't just military service; it's continued service. They didn't stop leading when they left the military. They kept showing up by mentoring new hires, speaking on panels, and creating pathways for others to follow.

Their leadership is precise. It's thoughtful. It's earned. And it's rooted in one belief: the next generation deserves more than a seat at the table, they deserve guidance on how to own the room.

These vets are the blueprint for what post-service purpose can look like. Not just rank and résumé—but reach. And if you're wondering how to make your own impact, start by asking: Who am I lifting as I lead?

FINAL CHAPTER: STUDY HALLS & SAFE HAVENS

Throughout this guide, you've met change-makers, mentors, disruptors, and builders—people who not only carved their own path into cybersecurity but also laid down bricks for the next person behind them. Now, in this final chapter, we turn our focus to the spaces and tools that make that journey a little less lonely and a lot more possible.

Study halls represent preparation—the resources that help you level up, skill up, and show up with confidence. Safe havens represent protection—those communities, programs, and platforms that offer refuge in an industry that can sometimes feel isolating, exclusionary, or overwhelming.

The resources in this chapter were thoughtfully curated and generously shared by the guests you've met in earlier chapters—people of color, women, veterans, neurodivergent professionals, and career switchers who know firsthand what it means to navigate a space where the default wasn't designed for you. They've lived the obstacles and the opportunities. They know what makes a difference.

And here's the truth: for many of us, success in cybersecurity not only comes from talent or tenacity, but also from access to networks, mentors, scholarships, prep materials, LinkedIn support groups, Slack channels, or that one webinar that finally clicked. It comes from someone saying, "Here's a space where you can learn, grow, and just be."

This chapter is for you—for those pushing through impostor syndrome, learning on the fly, or wondering if they belong. These resources are proof that you do belong, and know that there's a whole community of folks rooting for you to thrive.

So, explore. Share. Plug in. And remember: the dream is real, but we build it together.

CHAPTER 10

Cyber Career Advancement Guide

This guide offers organizations, study resources, and media created by and for underrepresented voices in cybersecurity. They are curated from podcast interviews, field leaders, and trusted sources.

Organizations & Nonprofits

1. BlackGirlsHack (BGH) — https://www.blackgirlshack.org/
2. BroadFutures — https://broadfutures.org/programs/
3. CyberMyte — https://cybermyte.io/
4. Cyversity — https://www.cyversity.org/
5. Direnzic Technology — https://www.direnzic.com/
6. Fortinet Veterans Program — https://www.fortinet.com/blog/industry-trends/fortinet-training-institute-helps-veterans-transition-into-cybersecurity
7. Minorities in Cybersecurity (MiC) — https://www.minoritiesincybersecurity.org/
8. Global Patch Gaming— https://www.globalpatchgaming.com/
9. Pierre's Tech Heads / BLT — https://www.pierrestechheads.com/
10. Professor Roger Cyber Lounge — https://linktr.ee/prcl.linktree
11. Raíces Cyber Org — https://www.raicescyber.org/
12. Repped In Tech — https://www.reppedin.tech/
13. Secure Diversity — https://www.securediversity.org/
14. The Cloud Family Foundation — http://www.thecloudfamily.org/
15. VetSec (Veterans in Cybersecurity) — https://www.veteransec.org/
16. WeGonnaLearnToday.com — https://www.wegonnalearntoday.com/
17. Women's Society of Cyberjutsu (WSC) — https://womenscyberjutsu.org/
18. Women in CyberSecurity (WiCyS) — https://www.wicys.org/

19. WiCyS Veteran Fellowship —
    https://www.wicys.org/initiatives/veteran-assistance/

Study & Training Resources

20. BlackGirlsHack Book Club — https://www.blackgirlshack.org/
21. Hacker in Heels — https://www.hackerinheels.com/
22. ThriveDX Bootcamps — https://thrivedx.com/
23. ThriveDX Cyber Empowerment Fund —
    https://thrivedx.com/cyber-empowerment-fund

Podcasts & YouTube Channels

24. Breaking Into Cybersecurity —
    https://podcasts.apple.com/us/podcast/breaking-into-
    cybersecurity/id1463136698
25. Cyber Coffee Hour —
    https://podcasts.apple.com/us/podcast/cyber-coffee-
    hour/id1752131544
26. Cyber Coffee Hour (Spotify) —
    https://creators.spotify.com/pod/show/cyber-coffee-hour
27. Cyber Explorers Podcast — https://soundcloud.com/user-
    898649155
28. Cyber Queens Podcast —
    https://podcasts.apple.com/us/podcast/the-cyber-queens-
    podcast/id1643732283

29. DEM Tech Folks Podcast —
   https://linktr.ee/developeverymind

30. DEM Tech Folks (Apple Podcasts) —
   https://podcasts.apple.com/ca/podcast/dem-tech-folks/id1680354042

31. Drafting Compliance Podcast (Spotify) —
   https://open.spotify.com/show/3CYNuCBk7EzH6FqjscVbVt

32. Kevtech IT Support — https://kevtechitsupport.com/

33. Kevtech IT Support (YouTube) —
   https://www.youtube.com/@KevTechITSupport

34. Direnzic Technology Consulting Group, LLC —
   https://www.youtube.com/channel/UC-VAbSxmxWZvDUz80nYPR_g

35. Stats On Stats Podcast — https://www.statsonstats.io/

36. Stats On Stats (Apple Podcasts) —
   https://podcasts.apple.com/us/podcast/stats-on-stats-podcast/id1720071250

37. The Other Side of the Firewall (YouTube) —
   https://www.youtube.com/@theothersideofthefirewallpod

38. The Other Side of the Firewall (Spotify) —
   https://open.spotify.com/show/7mXKrKmGrlKfFvyVjOGtKz

39. Women in Security Podcast —
   https://podcasts.apple.com/us/podcast/women-in-security-podcast/id1468319978

40. WiCyS YouTube Channel —
   https://www.youtube.com/@WomeninCyberSecurityWiCySorg

41. Women's Society of Cyberjutsu YouTube —
   https://www.youtube.com/c/WomensCyberjutsu12

Author Biography

Ryan Williams Sr. is a cybersecurity consultant, retired Air Force veteran, and CEO of RAM Cyber Consulting & Assessments, LLC. With over 22 years of experience, he specializes in GRC, vCISO services, and various risk management frameworks. Ryan is also a Principal Technology Risk Management professional in the financial sector and host of The Other Side of the Firewall podcast, which is syndicated on WDJY 99.1 FM in Atlanta and Fairfax Channel 10 Public Access. His work has been recognized by ISC2, Dark Reading, and CIO.com.

Next Steps

If this guide helped you, here's how you can pay it forward:

- Leave a review on Amazon or Goodreads
- Recommend the podcast to a friend or mentee
- Share the guide with someone exploring cyber
- Tag us online to share your thoughts

Connect with Me

Website: theothersideofthefirewall.com
Podcast: *The Other Side of the Firewall*
Email: theothersideofthefw@gmail.com
LinkedIn: www.linkedin.com/in/ryrysecurityguy
Business: RAM Cyber Consulting & Assessments, LLC.
Website: www.ramcyber.io

"Stay safe, stay secure." —Ryan Williams Sr.

www.ingramcontent.com/pod-product-compliance
Lightning Source LLC
Chambersburg PA
CBHW040925210326
41597CB00030B/5178